Bibliotheca Indo-Buddhica No.- 25

A Glossary of Buddhist Terms

A.C. MARCH

SRI SATGURU PUBLICATIONS
DELHI—INDIA

Distributed by:-
Indian Books Centre,
Exportors of Indological Books,
40/5, Shakti Nagar,
Delhi-110 007.
(India).

Published by:-

(C) **Sri Satguru Publications,**
Indological and Oriental Publishers,
40/5, Shakti Nagar,
Delhi-110 007.
(India).

Second and Revised Edition : London 1937
Third Edition : Delhi 1986

I.S.B.N. 81-7030-025-8

Printed in India at
Mohindra Offset Press,
Delhi-110 052.

ABBREVIATIONS.

A.F.M.	...	Awakening of Faith (Suzuki).
Ang. N.	...	Anguttara Nikaya.
A. P.	...	Abhidhamma Pitaka.
APC.	...	Analysis of Pali Canon.
B. ...	...	Buddhist.
B. A. C.	...	Buddhist Annual of Ceylon.
B. A. H.	...	Buddhist Annual of Hawaii.
B. E.	...	Buddhism in England.
B. L. B.	...	Buddhist Lodge Bibliography.
B. R.	...	Buddhist Review.
Bsm	...	Buddhism.
c. ...	...	circa (about).
cp.	...	compare.
Chin.	...	Chinese.
d. ...	...	died.
Dhp	...	Dhammapada.
Dial.	...	Dialogues of the Buddha (P.T.S.).
Dig. N.	...	Digha Nikaya.
e.g.	...	for example.
G. B.	...	Gospel of Buddha (Carus).
ib. ...	...	(ibidem) Same reference.
Jap.	...	Japanese.
Jat.	...	Jatakas.
J.P.T.S.	...	Journal Pali Text Society.
J.R.A.S.	...	Journal Royal Asiatic Society.
Khu. N.	...	Khuddaka Nikaya.
Lat. & Long.		are given approx. only. Sufficient to find site on map.
Maj. N.	...	Majjhima Nikaya.
M. ...	...	Mahayana.
Nanjio	...	Nanjio's Catalogue of Chinese Tripitaka.
o. p.	...	Out of Print.

P. ...	...	Pali.
P.T.S.	...	Pali Text Society.
QKM.	...	Questions of King Milinda.
q.v.	...	(quod vide) which see.
ref.	...	Refer to.
Rh. D.	...	Rhys Davids.
S. ...	...	Sutta.
S.B.E.	...	Sacred Books of the East.
Sk.	...	Sanskrit.
S. P.	...	Sutta Pitaka.
Sam. N.	...	Samyutta Nikaya.
sqq.	...	and following.
Tib.	...	Tibetan.
V. P.	...	Vinaya Pitaka.
v. ...	...	(vide) see.
W.B.	...	What is Buddhism? (Buddhist Lodge Publication).
Xtn	...	Christian.
Xty	...	Christianity.

BRIEF GLOSSARY OF BUDDHIST TERMS

ABHIDHAMMA (P): A commentarial division of the Buddhist Canon (v. Tipitaka), which deals with same subject-matter as Sutta Pitaka, but subjects it to analytical examination. Abhidhamma Pitaka consists of seven works: Dhammasangani, Vibhanga, Dhatukatha, Puggalapannati, Kathavatthu, Yamaka, and Patthana. (Ref. A.P.C. 9 & 18.)

ABHINNA (P): Serenity and Enlightenment of Mind. The Modes of Mystic Insight attained by the practice of Dhyana. (v. Dhyana; Jhana.)

ABSOLUTE: In primitive Buddhism an agnostic attitude towards metaphysical problems reigned, but as the transcendental experiences of the Arahats were pondered over, the problem of the nature of the goal led to speculation, and definite schools of philosophic thought came into existence. Hinayana inclines to a materialistic realism, Madhyamika to a mental realism, Yogacharya to the eternal evolution of a formative principle. In the later Mahayana mysticism rules. Tathata (translated "Suchness") is the Ultimate Reality, and as the fundamental essence of all Life, existence is neither purely phenomenal nor purely noumenal. Tathata is Eternal Being and Eternal Becoming, the Norm of Life and the Essence of Life. Immanent in Life, yet transcending its expression, existence moves towards ever more perfect expression of this ineffable and infinite Reality, so that we realize the truth of the assertion that not a single grain of sand exists which will not ultimately enter into Nirvana.

ADI-BUDDHA (Skt): In the sects of the Mahayana which have inclined to a theistic interpretation of the philosophical principles of the Dharma, Adi-Buddha is the primordial Buddha, the self-existent, unoriginated source of Universal Mind and Divine Manifestation. Its creative power is symbolised under form of five Dhyani Buddhas (q.v.), whose active aspects are personified under the Dhyani Bodhi-

BRIEF GLOSSARY OF BUDDHIST TERMS.

ABHIDHAMMA (P): A commentarial division of the Buddhist Canon (v. *Tipitaka*), which deals with same subject-matter as Sutta Pitaka, but subjects it to analytical examination. Abhidhamma Pitaka consists of seven works: *Dhammasangani, Vibhanga, Dhatukatha, Puggalapaññatti, Kathavatthu, Yamaka,* and *Patthana.* (Ref. APC. 9 & 18.)

ABHINNA (P): Serenity and Enlightenment of Mind. The Modes of Mystic Insight attained by the practice of Dhyana. (v. *Dhyana. Iddhis.*)

ABSOLUTE: In primitive Bsm an agnostic attitude towards metaphysical problems reigned, but as the transcendental experiences of the Arahats were pondered over, the problem of the nature of the goal led to speculation, and definite schools of philosophic thought came into existence. Hinayana inclines to a materialistic realism, Madhyamika to a mental realism, Yogacharya to the eternal evolution of a formative principle. In the later Mahayana mysticism rules. *Tathata* (translated " Suchness ") is the Ultimate Reality, and as the fundamental essence of all Life, existence is neither purely phenomenal nor purely noumenal. Tathata is Eternal Being and Eternal Becoming, the Norm of Life and the Essence of Life. Immanent in Life, yet transcending its expression, existence moves towards ever more perfect expression of this ineffable and infinite Reality, so that we realize the truth of the assertion that not a single grain of sand exists which will not ultimately enter into Nirvana.

ADI-BUDDHA (Sk): In the sects of the Mahayana which have inclined to a theistic interpretation of the philosophical principles of the Dhamma, Adi-Buddha is the primordial Buddha, the self-existent, unoriginated source of Universal Mind and Divine Ideation. Its creative power is symbolized under form of five Dhyani Buddhas (q.v.), whose active aspects are personified under the Dhyani Bodhisattvas, these in turn being represented on earth as the Buddhas of the *seven* Root Races of humanity. (There are seven Dhyani Buddhas actually, but names of five only are generally given.) Avalokitesvara is the Dhyani Bodhisattva of the present age and the Buddha Gautama his earthly reflex.

AGNOSTICISM: The Spencerian philosophic doctrine that man can never know the nature of Ultimate Reality. Bsm differs from Spencerian agnosticism in that it asserts an innate transcendental faculty in man which by elimination of all elements of "defilement" (*asavas*) may contemplate Reality and attain perfect knowledge and enlightenment—Nirvana (q.v.). v. *Creed of Buddha*, p. 170. Also *Japan: The Religion Interpreted*. L. Hearn.

AHIMSA (P): "Not hurting," compassion, esp. for animals. Both Buddhist and Jain lay great stress on virtue of *ahimsa*. First B. precept enjoins negative compassion by not taking life, and first of Four Sublime Moods (v. *Meditation*) inculcates positive compassion for all life. For accounts of influence of doctrine on B. Peoples, see Fielding Hall *Soul of a People*.

AJIVO (P): Mode of living, livelihood. *Samma Ajivo* is the Fifth step on the Eightfold Path (v. *Livelihood*).

AMARAVATI TOPE: Magnificent specimen of Buddhist art, discovered 1797 in Madras (N. 16, E. 80). Sculptures formed decorations of a stupa 138 feet in diameter, and an inner and outer rail surrounding it. Most of the sculptures were destroyed before the stupa was discovered, the specimens rescued being now in British Museum or Madras Museum. The work dates from c. 200 B.C. —300 A.D. and represents the intermediate stage between ancient Buddhist art and that of the Gandhara period, both symbol and figure being used to depict the Buddha. v. Burgess, *The Buddhist Stupas of Amaravati and Jaggayyapeta* (London, 1887).

AMITABHA (Sk) (Amida, Jap): The Buddha of Infinite Light. The Fourth of the Dhyani Buddhas (q.v.). The personification of compassion in its ultimate form. In the Pure Land sects of China and Japan, Amitabha is the intermediary between Supreme Reality and Mankind, and faith in him ensures rebirth in his Paradise (*Sukhavati*). Esoterically A. is Higher Self, and rebirth into his paradise is the awakening of the *Bodhicitta* in the heart of man. For Scriptures v. *Pure Land.*

ANAGAMIN (P): "Never Returner"; the third of the four stages on the Path. The anagamin does not return to earth after his death, but is reborn in the highest formless heavens and there attains arahatship (v. *Paths, Fetters*).

ANAGARIKA (homeless) DHARMAPALA (protector of the Law): Name used by Mr. D. H. Hewavitarne, a famous teacher, writer, organizer in Buddhist movement. Devoted life to Buddhist work at age 16, under advice of H. P. Blavatsky. Founder of Maha Bodhi Society, etc., and of Buddhist Mission in England. Entered Sangha, July, 1931, under name Sri Devamitta Dhammapala, died 1933.

ANANDA METTEYA: The name given to Charles Henry Allan Bennett in 1902 when he was ordained in Akyab, Burma, as a Bhikkhu. In 1908 he led a Mission to England to establish Buddhism as a living religion in the British Isles. Dr. Ernest Rost, Hon. Secretary of the International Buddhist Society which A. M. founded in Rangoon in 1903, prepared the way in England by founding the Buddhist Society of Great Britain and Ireland (Q.v.) A. M. returned to Burma after six months, but in 1914 was forced to return to England by ill-health. He died in March, 1923. (v. *The Development of Buddhism in England.* Humphreys, London, 1937.)

ANATTA (P): The doctrine of non-ego, one of the three characteristics of existence. All is *anatta, dukkha, anicca.* The doctrine of the non-separateness of all life. As applied to man it signifies that there is no ego or self in the five skandhas composing personality. "Put aside," the Buddha said, "that which is not you, your body, your sensations, your mental faculties, consciousness itself." The doctrine does not *deny* an ego or soul, as the Buddha when questioned refused so to deny it, but it means that although we are not wholly summed up in a "bundle of transitory states of becoming," yet the nature of that reality behind them can only be known by treading the Eightfold Path to the goal, and thereby realizing the transcendental unity in which all life is embraced. (v. *Ego, Self,* also ref. *W.B.*, pp, 42 & 100.)

ANGUTTARA NIKAYA: Fourth of the five Nikayas or collection of Discourses of Buddha into which *Sutta Pitaka* is divided. (v. APC. 8 & 17.)

ANICCA (P): Impermanence; one of the three characteristics of all existence: *anatta, dukkha, anicca.* The doctrine teaches that everything is subject to the law of cause and effect, is the creation of preceding causes and is in its turn a cause of after effects. There is in existence, therefore, no stable being, but only an ever-becoming flux. This is a basic teaching of the Dhamma, and a realization of its truth is essential to the attainment of Right Knowledge and Enlightenment. (v. *W.B.* 23.)

ANIMAL: Rebirth as animal is often recorded in Buddhist writings, but is accepted only figuratively, in sense of displaying animal vices; gluttony, stupidity, etc. (v. Intro. *Tibetan Book of the Dead.* Evans Wentz.)

ANNIHILATION: Misunderstanding of Anatta doctrine has led to idea of annihilation as goal of Buddhist endeavour. The only kind of annihilation taught by Buddha was that of the skandhas which form the evanescent part of man. When the Arhat enters Nirvana he passes "beyond the vision of gods and men," losing objective existence but retaining subjective being. (v. *Nirvana. Anatta.* Also *Creed of Buddha,* p. 217.)

ARHAT (P), ARHANT (Sk) (Arhan and Rahat also found): The Worthy One. One who has traversed the Eightfold Path to the Goal, eliminated the 10 Fetters and the 4 Asavas which bind to existence, and on the death of the physical body attains Nirvana. Arahatship: the Goal of the Path (Hinayana). (Spelled: *Arhat, Arahat, Arahan, Rahat;* (Chin.) *Yingkong,* also *Lohan;* (Jap.) *Arakan;* (Tib.) *Dgrabchom-pa.* cp. *Bodhisattva.* (v. *Early Buddhist Theory of Man Perfected.* Horner, London, 1937.)

ART: Bsm. fostered art wherever it penetrated, notably in architecture and sculpture. v. *Architecture, Rupa, Ajanta.* Members of Sangha often skilled artists. Example: Asvaghosa, poet and musician. Aim of B. art is endeavour to express inner reality of which the form is expression. Foucher, *Beginnings of Buddhist Art* (Trsl. Thomas), and v. *Amaravati, Gandhara.*

ARUPA (P): Formless, incorporeal. *Arupalokas*: The highest heaven worlds, where form cognizable by the five senses does not exist, being purely mental. *Aruparaga*: attachment to the formless heaven worlds; the 7th Fetter on the Path. (v. *Fetters.*)

ARYAN: Arya, âriya; noble. Name given to the Indo-European languages; taken from Aryans who conquered Punjab and attained supremacy in India. *Ariya atthanga magga;* Noble Eightfold Path (q.v.). *Ariyadhana*: The Noble Treasures: faith, morality, modesty, conquest of evil, knowledge, self-denial, wisdom. *Ariyasaccani*: The Four Noble Truths: *Dukkha, Samudaya, Nirodha, Marga* (q.v.). Buddha called his doctrine "Noble," as worthy of Aryans (racial), and conducive to nobility (in conduct).

ASAVAS (P): Mental intoxication, defilement. The four asavas are: *kama-*, sensuality; *bhava-*, lust of life; *dittha-*, delusion; and *avijja-*, ignorance (of nature of life). Erroneous ideas which intoxicate mind so that it cannot contemplate pure truth and attain enlightenment. Total freedom from *asavas* = arhatship.

ASCETICISM: As practised for gaining magical powers or propitiating gods is essentially selfish. In First Sermon Buddha condemned extreme asceticism as ignoble and useless, and taught Middle Way between self-mortification and allurements of senses. Only asceticism Bsm permits is abstinence and bodily self-control as aids to mental self-control, practise of virtue and altruism: i.e., renunciation of temporary pleasure for permanent happiness. Rules governing layman are Five Precepts always, three additional for special occasions. For bhikkhus Ten Precepts plus 227 *Vinaya* (disciplinary) Rules, (v. *Patimokkha.*) Buddhist ideal the arhat, not the ascetic. Scrip. refs: *APC.* 2, 8, 25, 38, 45, 46, 70, 73, 74, 184.

ASOKA (the Great): Emperor of India (c. 270-230 B.C.), grandson of Chandragupta, founder of Maurya (peacock) dynasty. Great Buddhist ruler. Convert to Bsm from Hinduism (*ajivika* sect): earnestly practised *dhamma* within his empire and spread it outside. Sent his son Mahinda, and daughter Sanghamitta, to Ceylon, who converted ruler and people to Bsm.

Asoka, renowned for his "Edicts," engraved on rocks and pillars throughout his empire. Most famous of these records is Bhabra Edict (q.v.) and Rummindei Pillar (q.v.) recording birthplace of Buddha.

He abolished war in his empire and restricted the slaughter of animals and hunting. Built hospitals for man and beast. Respected the good in every creed. H. G. Wells classes him amongst the six greatest men known to history. Known also as Dharmasoka and Piyadasi. Refs. v. *Asoka*, Mookerji (1928), *Asoka*, V. Smith, also *B.E. II.* 15, 200.

ASVAGHOSA: One of the most famous B. philosophers. "The Buddhist Origen." Lived about 600 years after the *parinirvana*. Synthesized essence of Mahayana teaching in *Mahayanasraddhotpada Sastra.* (Trsl. Suzuki, *Awakening of Faith in the Mahayana.*) Was accomplished musician and poet. Wrote famous Life of Buddha in verse, *Buddha Caritakavya* (trsl. *Fo-sho-hing-tsan-king. S.B.E.* vols. 19 & 49.)

Teaching: Phenomenal world is actualization under limits of space-time of *Tathata* (symbolized as Amitabha). Whole of existence, therefore, "perfumed" with nature of the Real. Faith in Grace of Amitabha brings this innate Reality in man (*Bodhicitta*) into fruition, with consequent Enlightenment and Liberation from rebirth.

ATHEISM: Bsm is atheistic in the sense that it does not recognize or rely on a creative being in the sense of a Supreme Personal Deity, but is not philosophically atheistic, as it does not deny Ultimate Reality. (v. *Agnosticism*, and Holmes *Creed of Buddha*, p. 200 sqq.)

ATISA: Native of India (c. 1030 A.D.) Reformer of Lamaism of Tibet. Founded Order called Kah-dam, which purged Lamaism of grosser elements. Four hundred years later Tsong-khapa (q.v.) reformed kah-dam, renaming it Ge-lug-pa. Known as Yellow Hat sect, is now most powerful body in Tibet. Atisa wrote and trsl. many works. d. 1052 A.D. at Ne-t'ang, near Lhasa.

ATMAN (Sk) (atta P): The Supreme SELF; Universal Consciousness; Ultimate Reality. The Divine Monad in man, degraded into idea of an entity dwelling in the heart of each man, the thinker of his thoughts, and doer of his deeds, and after death dwelling in bliss or misery according to deeds done in the body. For Buddhist attitude to Atman conception (v. *anatta*).

ATONEMENT (Vicarious atonement): Primitive Bsm. knows nothing of vicarious atonement. Bsm. individualistic religion; each must work out his own salvation. We may help each other by thought, word and deed, but cannot bear results or take over consequences of another's errors or misdeeds. In certain Mahayana sects theistic interpretation of *anatta* doctrine has produced doctrine of Bodhisattvas who help humanity by renouncing benefit of their accumulated store of " merit," and " handing it over " to credit of bad karma of humanity. This has further developed into salvation by grace of Amida by calling on his name. If, however, atonement is understood as an " at-one-ment " with the Law of the universe (*Dharmakaya* q.v.), then it may be called a Buddhist principle. (v. *Parivarta, Amitagha, Tariki.*)

ATTAVADA (P): The doctrine or belief in a persistent soul or self. One of the *upadanas* in the Chain of Causation. Cp. *sakkayaditthi* (the belief in a self).

AUTHORITY: (1) There is no " authority " in Bsm in the sense of one who gives forth doctrine which must be accepted, or who gives authoritative explanation of doctrine. Each Buddhist is his own authority, in the sense that he must learn the Truth for himself, by study, self-discipline and practice (v. *W.B.* 163, 175). (2) No written teaching or scripture is authoritative in the sense of binding. See Buddha's advice to Kalamans. (*Ang.N.* I., 188, also v. *W.B.* 182.) (3) So-called " authorities " on Bsm are authorities only in the sense that being experts in the languages, Pali, Sk., Jap., Tib., Chinese, they are able to translate to the best of their ability the *letter* of the teaching. They are not necessarily competent to expound spiritual meaning of it. Only a Buddhist who lives the Law can understand the Law.

AUM (Sk): Mantra to Avalokitesvara: *Aum mani padme hum!* Symbolizes the self-generative creative cosmic force, operating alike in the Universe and in Man. The Cosmos self-creative: man his own creator and saviour. (v. *Creation, Nidanas.* Also spelt OM!)

AVALOKITESVARA (Sk): Also called Padmapani. Lit.: "The Lord which is seen"; that is to say: The Divine SELF as perceived by *Buddhi,* the faculty of intuition. The Higher Self, in the Cosmos and in Man. The Bodhisattva of the Dhyani Buddha Amitabha. Personification of the self-generative creative cosmic force. (v. AUM! also *Lotus* (his emblem).)

AVATAMSAKA SUTRA (or Gandavyuha): Important M. scripture. Teaches doctrine of the Absolute Buddha, the Trikaya, and the Ten Stages of Bodhisattvahood. Epitomised version in "*Eastern Buddhist,*" vol. one.

AVIJJA (P) AVIDYA (Sk): Ignorance; lack of enlightenment; the fundamental root of evil, and the ultimate cause of the desire which creates the *dukkha* of existence. It is the nearest approach to "original sin," known to Bsm. Its total elimination, resulting in perfect enlightenment, is Goal of Buddhist Path. Ignorance is first of the Twelve Nidanas or Links in the Chain of Causation: *first* because it is the primary cause of existence. It is the *last* of the Ten Fetters: last because until full enlightenment is attained there still remains some degree of error or ignorance. The final removal of the veil of ignorance (v. *Asavas*), reveals supreme Truth—Nirvana. (v. *W.B.* 137.)

BARDO: The intermediate state between death in the physical world and rebirth, according to the teachings of Tibetan Buddhism. It is a purely mental state, and its conditions depend on the nature of the personality creating them. For detailed description, see *Tibetan Book of. the Dead,* and *Mahatma Letters.*

BELIEF: *Sammaditthi,* the first step on the Noble Path is often translated "right belief." More correct rendering is "right understanding." Belief, in Bsm, must result from the mental apprehension based on reason, not on mere mental acquiescence to the authority of another. Belief is confirmed by experience, for only by living Truth can one *know* and become enlightened. (v. *Faith. Eightfold Path. Wisdom.*)

BHAVA (Sk & P): Philosophical term signifying "becoming," a state of existence (all existence being states of "becoming"), a life. In the Causal Chain (v. *Nidanas*), *bhava* is the link between *upadana* (clinging to life), and *jati* (rebirth). (v. *Bhavana.*)

BHAVANA (Sk & P): Lit. a "making-to-become." Self-development by any means, but especially by the method of mind-control, concentration and meditation. Continued practice of *bhavana* produces the Four Sublime States or *Brahma Viharas* (q.v.) (v. *W.B.* 138-143.)

BHIKKHU (P) BHIKSHU (Sk): A member of the Buddhist *Sangha* (q.v.); variously translated monk, mendicant, friar, almsman, priest: all of which convey wrong ideas. A bhikkhu is one who has devoted himself to the task of following the Path by renunciation of the distractions of worldly affairs. He relies for his sustenance upon the gifts of the lay disciples, being under no obligation to give anything in return, but often devoting part of his time to secular and religious teaching. A bhikkhu keeps the Ten Precepts and his daily life is governed by 227 rules (v. *Patimokkha*). Feminine equivalent *bhikkhuni.*

BHUTATATHATA: See *Tathata.*

BIBLIOGRAPHY, A BUDDHIST: Compiled by Arthur C. March. 260 pp., medium 8vo. Published by the Buddhist Lodge, London, in 1935, at

21s., since reduced to 7s. 6d. The most comprehensive Buddhist Bibliography in print. Over 2,000 items detailed and classified under authors, with a detailed subject index. Referred to as B.L.B. (Buddhist Lodge Bibliography).

BIMBISARA: King of Magadha at time of Buddha. Built city of Rajagaha. Convert to Bsm, and presented Veluvana (Bamboo Grove) to Buddha for use of Sangha. Was dethroned and murdered by his son Ajatasattu. Not to be confused with Bindusara.

BINDUSARA: (298-270 B.C.) Son of Chandragupta, founder of Maurya Dynasty. Father of Asoka.

BIRTH: The arising of a state of being in any sphere of existence, the effect of anterior conditions. No coming of existence from previously non-existent: creation *ex nihilo* inconceivable to a Buddhist. Birth into physical state is union of pre-existing character and consciousness with the physical vehicle in the womb of the mother, not the ejection of the fœtus. (v. *Life. Jati.*)

BIRTH AND DEATH: The realm of Samsara (becoming) as contrasted with *Nirvana* (Being). In M. philosophy, birth and death is the manifestation or self-realization under the limits of conditionality of that which is in essence transcendental and eternal—*Tathata* (q.v.).

BLAVATSKY, Helena Petrovna: Born, Russia, midnight 30/31st July, 1831. Co-founder with Col. Olcott of Theosophical Society: author of *Isis Unveiled, Secret Doctrine, Key to Theosophy, Voice of the Silence,* etc. Declared herself a Buddhist at Galle (Ceylon) in 1880, and inspired the Buddhist revival in Ceylon. d. 8th May, 1891, London. Accusations of deceit made by agent of S.P.R. were withdrawn; and apology for libel in New York "Sun," July, 1890, was made September, 1892. (v. *The Real H. P. Blavatsky*, W. Kingsland).

BOAR'S FLESH: Owing to a mis-translation of the Pali word *sukaramaddava,* the story has become current that the Buddha died from eating rich boar's flesh. There is some doubt as to exact meaning of word, but all authorities agree that it cannot mean "flesh of boars." It is now usually translated "boar's delight," and is identified with a kind of truffle found in N. India and known as sukara-kanda (boar's root, *Tuber indicum*). (v. *Dial. ii.* 137, and *Buddhist Scriptures,* Thomas, p. 109.)

BODHI (Sk): Enlightenment. The spiritual condition of a Buddha or Bodhisattva. The fruit of *bodhi* is *prajñâ* and *karunâ* (q.v.). Bodhi is the name given to the highest state of *samadhi* (q.v.) in which the mind is awakened and illuminated. (v. *buddhi.*)

BODHICITTA (Sk): Wisdom-heart. The especial characteristic of the Bodhisattva, *bodhi* and *citta* being synonymous for the perfected qualities of *prajñâ* and *karunâ.* Nagarjuna, in his *Treatise on the Transcendality of Bodhicitta,* says that the Bodhisattva, by renunciation of all claim to results of individual meritorious deeds, practises compassion to the highest degree of perfection by working ever in the worlds of birth and death for the ultimate enlightenment of humanity. (v. *Bodhisattva.*)

BODHIDHARMA: Famous Indian Buddhist of 6th c. A.D., who established Zen School in China, where he is classed as the first of the six great Chinese Patriarchs. He aimed at simplification of doctrine, and placed no reliance on scriptures, but taught awakening of Buddha-nature within by direct perception. B. was 28th Patriarch of Dhyani School in India. Chinese name Pu-ti-ta-mo or Tamo. Jap. Daruma. (v. *Zen. Dhyana.*)

BODHISATTA (P), BODHISATTVA (Sk): One whose "being" or "essence" (*sattva*) is *bodhi,* that is, the wisdom resulting from direct perception of Truth, with the compassion awakened thereby. (v. *Bodhi.*)

In Hinayana, an aspirant for Buddha-hood: the Buddha is described in Jataka account of his former lives as *the Bodhisatta.*

In Mahayana, the Bodhisattva is the ideal of the Path as contrasted with the Arahat of the Hinayana. He is one who, having practised the Ten Paramitas and attained Enlightenment, renounces Nirvana in order to help humanity on its pilgrimage. The Bodhisattvas are often called "Buddhas of Compassion," as love in action guided by wisdom is their aim.

The *Dhyani Bodhisattvas* (of the theistic schools of M.) are hypostatic personifications of the attributes of the Dhyani Buddhas, who are in their turn the objective aspects of the self-creative forces of the primal reality, Adi-Buddha (q.v.) (v. *Paramitas, parivarta.*)

BODHI TREE: The tree under which the Buddha attained Enlightenment at Buddha Gaya. A kind of fig tree: popularly called Pipal Tree: scientific name *Ficus religiosa.* Also called *Assattha Tree.*

BON (Tib.): (*Bön; Bhon; Bonbo; Boa-ho*). The indigenous (pre-Buddhist) religion of Tibet; identical with the Shamanism of Mongolia. Introduced, according to Tibetan tradition by Gsen-rabs (5c. A.D.; but probably much earlier). It is a debased form of Tantricism (spiritualism mixed with phallic worship). There are two sects, Black and White. Former very debased; latter, influenced by Bsm, less degraded. Use reversed swastika as symbol.

"BRITISH BUDDHIST": Organ of Buddhist Mission in England. Founded October, 1926. Publication ceased, December, 1934. (v. *Wheel, The.*)

BRITISH MAHA BODHI SOCIETY: Founded in July, 1926, by the Anagarika Dharmapala (q.v.) at Foster House, 86, Madeley Road, Ealing, as a branch of the parent Society founded by him at Calcutta in 1891. Published the *British Buddhist* in October, 1926, replaced by *The Wheel* in January, 1935. Moved to present headquarters, 41, Gloucester Road, N.W.1, in February, 1928. Meetings held every Sunday at 6 p.m. for lecture and discussion. Nearest station Camden Town. v. *The Development of Buddhism in England.* Humphreys. Pub. Buddhist Lodge. 1937. 3s.

BUDDHA: A title, not the name of a person. Derived from root *budh,* "to know," it means one who knows in the sense of having become one with the highest object of knowledge, Supreme Truth. There have been many Buddhas in the past (Pali scriptures mention 24) and there will be others in the future. (v. *Maitreya.*) Gotama, the historical founder of Buddhism (q.v.), was born near Kapilavatthu, N. India (100 miles N.E. Benares). Date of his birth according to Hinayana School of Bsm was 623 B.C.; according to modern historical research 563 B.C. The birthplace is marked by pillar erected by Asoka. (v. *Rummindei.*) Birth is celebrated on Full Moon day of month *Vaisekha* (April—May) (v. *Wesak.*)

The historicity of the Buddha Gotama is not seriously questioned. The strongest evidence is in his recorded Teachings, and in the Order he founded, which has been described as the "greatest monastic order known to history." (v. *Sangha.*)

The best "Life" is Brewster's *Life of Gotama the Buddha;* compiled exclusively from the Pali Canon. (1926.) The *Lalitavistara* (on which Arnold's *Light of Asia* is based), and *Fo-sho-hing-tsan-king* (*S.B.E.* xix) are overlaid with myth and legend.

BUDDHACHARITA: (or *Buddhacharita-kâvya*) is the Sanskrit title of a poem ascribed to Asvaghosa. It is a life of the Buddha, but contains much of the legendary matter which collected around the historical facts. The work was translated into Chinese by Dharmaraksha (c. 420 A.D.). A translation from the original Sanskrit by E. B. Cowell is given in volume 49 *S.B.E.* (*Buddhist Mahayana Sutras*), and from the Chinese by Beal, in volume 19 *S.B.E.* (*Fo-sho-hing-tsan-king*).

BUDDHA GAYA (Bodh Gaya): One of the most venerated places of Bsm: the place where the Buddha attained Enlightenment. Spot marked by Bo-tree and Temple, six miles from Gaya (approx. 24 N. 85 E.).

BUDDHAGHOSA: (Lit. "Voice of Buddha.") Name of several B. writers. Notably great Buddhist scholar born N. India early 5th c. A.D., who translated Sinhalese Commentaries into Pali and wrote Visuddhi Magga (q.v.), and other works, including Commentaries on whole of Pitakas. (v. *Life and Work of Buddhaghosa*, by B. C. Law (Calcutta, 1923), and *Buddhaghosauppatti*.)

BUDDHARUPA: An image of the Buddha. For about 500 years after the Parinibbana, the person of the Buddha was considered too holy to be depicted in the form of an image. At Sanchi, for instance, the symbols of the vacant throne or the footprint are used, at Armaravati (2nd c. A.D.) both symbolic and actual representation were used, (v. *Gandhara*.) Buddharupas represent the Blessed One as seated, standing, or recumbent (lying on the right side). The standing and recumbent are rare. There are three customary attitudes for the seated figure: (1) The "witness" attitude. The left hand lies flat upon the lap, palm upwards; the right hand is stretched downwards over the right knee, the palm being towards the body. The Buddha is calling upon the Earth to "witness" his right to the title of Tathagata, and it responded "with a roar like thunder" (*Jat.* i, 74). (2) The "meditation" attitude. The crossed hands lie flat in the lap with palms upturned, the right resting upon the left. (3) The "teaching" attitude. The right arm is half raised to bring the hand on a level with the breast, with the palm outwards, the second and third fingers being usually half closed; the left hand hangs by the side or supports the robe.

In Mahayana countries a variety of other forms are used. Rupas of Bodhisattvas are also common, *e.g.*, Kwannon, Avalokitesvara, Maitreya, Jizo, Amitabha, etc. See article *Images in Bsm. B.R.*, vol. vi, p. 81 sqq. The rupa is used in Bsm only as a focus for meditating on the attributes of the being depicted, not as an object of worship.

BUDDHI (Sk): The vehicle of Enlightenment (*Bodhi* q.v.)—*i.e.*, the *faculty* of supreme understanding as distinct from the understanding itself. The sixth principle in the sevenfold constitution of man taught in the esoteric schools of Buddhism, and as such the link between the Ultimate Reality and the Mind (*Manas*).

BUDDHISM: The name given to the Teachings of Gautama the Buddha (q.v.), but usually called by his followers the *Buddha Dhamma* (q.v.). Founded by the Buddha (c. 560-480 B.C.) and established by him in N.W. India, adopted by the Emperor Asoka as the religion of his empire, and introduced by him into Ceylon and neighbouring countries, it spread rapidly all over the East, eventually becoming the dominant religion of the world. Although it has declined in the land of its birth it still numbers over 300 millions of followers. (Biblio. *What is Buddhism?* The Buddhist Lodge, London, 3/-.)

BUDDHISM IN ENGLAND: First B. Mission to England landed April, 1908, led by Bhikkhu Ananda Metteya (Allan Bennett). Received by Buddhist Society of Great Britain and Ireland, founded November, 1907, by Dr. Ernest Rost and others, with Professor Rhys Davids as President. Buddhist Review, founded 1909, ceased 1922. Buddhist League, founded 1923, by Francis Payne, to replace moribund Buddhist Society of Great Britain and Ireland, which was formally wound up 1925. Buddhist Lodge, founded November, 1924, becoming Buddhist Lodge, London, in 1926. Its journal, *Buddhism in England*, founded May, 1926. Buddhist Mission, founded by Anagarika Dharmapala at Ealing, July, 1926; removed 1928 to 41, Gloucester Road, N.W.1. *British Buddhist*, founded as their journal 1926, replaced in January, 1935, by *The Wheel*. Students' Buddhist Association, founded 1927. Young Men's Buddhist Association, founded 1929 (v. *The Development of Buddhism in England*. Christmas Humphreys. Pub. Buddhist Lodge, London, 1937).

"BUDDHISM IN ENGLAND": *The Journal of Oriental Philosophy and Religion*, published by the Buddhist Lodge, London. Founded May, 1926. Every 2 months, May—April = 6 issues yearly. 1/6 each issue, or 7/6 p.a.

BUDDHIST: Nominally, one born into the Buddhist religion, or one who accepts Buddhism as his religion by public recitation of "Pansil" (q.v.) Actually, one who studies, disseminates and endeavours to live the fundamental principles of the Buddha-dhamma. (v. *W.B.*, pp, 7, 61, 104, 209, 214.)

BUDDHIST ANNUAL OF CEYLON: Published at Wesak each year by Bastian & Co., Colombo, from 1920 to 1932. Each issue contained from 80 to 120 pages, and consisted of articles on the doctrine and history of Buddhism, and its progress to-day. It was well illustrated with reproductions of Buddhist architecture and works of art, and with portraits of notable persons in the Buddhist Movement.

BUDDHIST ANNUAL OF HAWAII: (Correct title: *Hawaiian Buddhist Annual*). Published at Wesak each year by The Hongwanji Buddhist Mission, Honolulu, from 1930 to 1934, excepting 1933. Each issue contained about 130 pages and included articles on Buddhism and its mission to the world to-day.

BUDDHIST LEAGUE. See *Buddhism in England.*

BUDDHIST LODGE, LONDON: Founded as Lodge of Theosophical Society, November, 1924; seceded and became independent organization October, 1926. (See *B.E.*, vol. I, p. 121.) Objects: To form a nucleus of such persons as are prepared to study, disseminate, and endeavour to live the fundamental principles of Buddhism. Meetings: fortnightly Monday evenings, 7.15, at present Headquarters: 37, South Eaton Place, London, S.W.1. (Bus routes 11 and 39 pass near).

BUDDHIST MAHAYANA SUTRAS: Title of volume 49 *S.B.E.* Contains translations of: The *Buddha charita-kâvya* of Asvaghosa, by Cowell: The Larger *Sukhavati-vyuha;* the Smaller *Sukhavati-vyuha;* the *Vajracchedika;* the Larger *Prajñâpâramitâ-hridaya-sutra;* and the Smaller *Prajñâ pâramitâ-hridaya-sutra,* all by Max Müller: and the *Amitâyur-dhyâna-sutra,* by J. Takakusu.

BUDDHIST SOCIETY OF GREAT BRITAIN AND IRELAND (v. *Buddhism in England*).

BURMA: Buddhism first introduced by missionaries of King Asoka about 240 B.C. Mahayana later introduced by King Kanishka (c. 100 A.D.). Buddhaghosa visited Burma about 450 A.D. and firmly established religion there, since which time it has not ceased to be prevailing religion. Burma has consistently held important place in interpretation of Pali scriptures, esp. Abhidhamma, and has produced works of high merit. For centuries bhikkhus from Siam and Ceylon have visited Burma to study its commentaries on the Abhidhamma. (Ref.: *Soul of a People,* Fielding Hall; *The Burman,* J. G. Scott; *The Burman, his Life and Notions,* Shwe Yoe; *Pilgrimage of Bsm,* Pratt.)

CAMBODIA: Ancient seat of Khmer civilization, now kingdom under French protection.

Bounded by Siam, Annam, Cochin-China, and Gulf of Siam. Buddhism introduced about 5th c. completely subdued Brahmanism by 12th c. Formerly tinged with Mahayanism, now pure Hinayana. Capital Phnom-Penh has "National Institute for study of Bsm of Lesser Vehicle," opened in 1930. Has many wonderful Buddhist ruins and temples, including famous Angkor Wat.

CANON: Only Canon recognized by Hinayana School is the Tipitaka or Three Baskets (q.v.). This is supposed to have been established at Council of Asoka held c. 250 B.C., but was not committed to writing until c. 100 B.C. Mahayana School accepts Tipitaka as translated into Chinese, Japanese, Tibetan, etc., but adds other works such as *Saddharma Pundarika,* etc., and works relating to special tenets of sect. (See Sects.) The Tibetan Canon (Ka-gyur or Kanjur), comprises the Tipitaka, the nine great "Dharmas," the *Parinirvana Sutra,* and a number of Tantric works. The commentary (Tan-gyur or Tanjur) is an encyclopædia of lore or metaphysics, art, astrology, etc., with commentaries and texts by Nagarjuna, Tsong-khapa and other Masters.

CASTE: Class distinctions, dependent mainly on Aryan or non-Ayran birth or on occupation, prevailed at time of Buddha, but caste system later development. No class distinctions in Sangha: e.g., Upali the barber, one of the despised trades, was superior of Kshattriya nobles Ananda and Devadatta, superiority depending on length of time since ordination.

Note: Sunita, an outcaste: Sati, fisherman, one of the ignoble trades: Nanda, cowherd. Slaves admitted under consent of masters: Punna, slave-girl, an example. Outside Sangha, virtuous character only insignia of nobility. For Suttas dealing with subject, see *APC*. Subject Index p. 14. Rh.D. exhaustively treats in Intro. *Ambattha S.* (*Dial.* I, 96).

CAUSALITY: The doctrine that the law of causality reigns in the phenomenal worlds of existence is a fundamental one. No phenomenon (*dhamma*) arises without appropriate cause, therefore no " miracle " is possible. By creating suitable cause any effect may be produced, for all entities have causal efficacy according to their specific mental development and are not purely effects of causes external to themselves. (v. *Creation. Karma.*)

CEYLON OR LANKA: Ancient name Taprobane. Converted Bsm by son and daughter of Asoka c. 252 B.C. Stronghold of Bsm for many centuries, but had periods of decline and the teaching became almost extinct on several occasions, being revived by bhikkhus from Siam and Burma, who founded Siamese and Burmese sects. Almost exterminated by forced conversions under Portuguese rule, revived under Dutch and British rule, last revival being that by Col. Olcott in 1880. Always consistently Hinayana in doctrine. Present sects Siamese, Ramanya (rigid in doctrine and discipline), Amarapura (more liberal in views). v. *Romantic Ceylon.* Bassett. London, 1929, 7/6.

CHAITYA: P. & Sk. from *chitâ* "a funeral pile." Any kind of tumulus raised over remains of the dead. In Buddhism practically synonymous with *dagaba, stupa,* or *tope,* but the latter are rather the architectural terms, and chaitya the religious term. The term *chaitya* is also given by modern archæologists to the rock-hewn temples found in India. Tib. *chorten* or *dungten.* (v. *Dagoba.*)

CHINA: Buddhism was introduced into Chinese empire in reign of Emperor Ming-Ti, year 67 A.D., by two Indian bhikkhus, Kasyapa Matanga and Dharmaraksha, the White Horse Monastery built to accommodate them existing to-day. It made rapid progress, eventually becoming the dominant religion, although never supplanting Tâoism and Confucianism. Many schools of Buddhist thought developed and flourished, but the two predominating schools were the Ch'an (Jap. Zen) and Pure Land, or Amidist. Every phase of Chinese Bsm may be included under one or other of these, and even these two are not fundamentally at variance. Zen is to the educated what the Amida doctrines are to the unlearned, one being the method of experiencing immediately and in ordinary life the Reality which the other venerates under the concrete mental concepts of the Bodhisattva Amida and his Paradise of Bliss.

Religious leaders of high intellectual and moral attainments, like Tai Hsü and Ouyang, are reviving Bsm amongst the educated classes.

Best work is *Buddhist China,* by R. F. Johnston. See also Pratt's *Buddhist Pilgrimage.* (v. *Amitabha. Kwan-Yin. Pure Land. Zen.*)

CHRISTIANITY: Superficially there is a wide difference between Xty and original Bsm, although Xty as generally understood is in many ways identical with Pure Land Bsm, q.v. The difference is that both popular Xty and Pure Land Bsm deem man incapable of attaining salvation through his own efforts. Salvation must therefore be attained through faith in the redeeming power of Christ (or Amida), and this faith can only come through acceptance of the Grace of God which is offered freely to all men, whether saints or sinners. Original Bsm, on the other hand, while not denying the existence of a God or gods, taught that man could only be enlightened through his own efforts because he had only himself to blame for his ignorance. Fundamentally, however, these two views are not opposed. While they are theologically different, they are psychologically the same, for both involve a letting-go or surrender of "self." Both agree that man binds himself by clinging to himself, and that when he lets go he falls into the hands of God, or, in B. terms, realizes his true and original state which is free and pure.

CHRONOLOGY: Dates of historical events are given under appropriate subject headings. The Buddhist Era commences with the Parinirvana of the Buddha, which, according to the records of the Southern School, took place in 543 B.C.; Wesak 1937 A.D., therefore, ushered in the year 2481 B.E. Modern investigation tends to place the date about 60 years later, i.e., *circa* 563 for the birth and 483 for the Parinirvana. (See *J.R.A.S.*, January, 1909, article by J. F. Fleet: "The Day on which the Buddha died.") A. B. Keith and E. J. Thomas, amongst many other authorities, accept Fleet's date, 563—483 B.C. The Northern School place the date considerably earlier, Chinese Buddhists usually accepting 973 B.C. for the P.N. An effort was made for the year 1934 A.D. to be agreed upon by the Buddhists of all countries as 2500 B.E.

CITTA (Sk): The "heart" or focus of man's emotional nature plus its intellectual expression. *Bodhicitta* is the mind (heart) purified and guided by wisdom. Also understood in Yoga as "mind-stuff" or the substance in which thoughts take form.

COMPASSION: (P. *dana, karuna, metta.*) Lit. "to suffer with," compassion is the supreme Buddhist virtue, being based on the fundamental principle of the unity of all life. The second of the Four Sublime Moods—*karuna*, identifying oneself with the suffering of others and so creating active pity (*metta*)—this is the only form of vicarious sacrifice known to Buddhism. (v. *Ahimsa, Bodhisattva.*)

CONSCIENCE: Buddhism knows nothing of an "inner monitor" implanted by deity as an infallible guide to right conduct. "Conscience" is a quality of the mind resulting from past experience. Therefore, one's state of moral development depends on one's response to experience in past lives, and in the present life. There is no absolute right and wrong, there is gradual growth towards the highest morality—utter unselfishness.

CONSCIOUSNESS, in Buddhism comprises every stage of awareness from the simplest response to outside stimuli to the intuitive processes of pure mind. Consciousness is divided into two great classes: Phenomenal (*manoviññana*) and Transcendental (*alayaviññana*). The former is the relation between subject and object and the inferences drawn therefrom. It depends for its expression on the sense organs and mind (*ayatani*), and is therefore personal. The latter is independent of sense organs and of the relation of subject and object. The action of the former is ratiocinative, of the latter intuitive. These two aspects are united in an ultimate identity, of course, the nature of which is naturally incomprehensible to the normal mind, but which can and will be realized as the goal of the Eightfold Path is attained. The dhyanic consciousness, culminating in samadhi, represents the union of the two aspects of consciousness, in which individual consciousness is not lost, but is transcended in the union with universal consciousness. (v. *Dhyana, Samadhi, Mind.*)

CONTEMPLATION: Meditation involving the experience of *samadhi*, q.v. These are essentially supra-mental, in that the mind is illuminated and performs its function without the ratiocinative processes of conscious thought. This is recognized as the highest stage of conscious union with Reality, by both Buddhist and Christian mystics. (v. *dhyana, samadhi.*)

COUNCILS: The 1st C. was held at Rajagaha immediately after the *parinibbana* of the Buddha. It was presided over by Kasyapa, and lasted seven months. The Scriptures, as they then existed, were recited by all, Ananda leading with the doctrinal part, Upali with the part relating to discipline. The 2nd (and 2a) was held at Vaisali about 100 years later, to uphold the original teachings and the discipline of the Sangha. As a minority upheld the original teachings, the majority seceded and held a rival Council (2a): from this schism came the 18 sects of the Hinayana School. This Council lasted eight months. The 3rd was held in the 18th year of Asoka's reign (c. 250 B.C.) at Pataliputra (Patna). Here the Canon was fixed, although not written down until about 150 years later in Ceylon. This lasted nine months. The 4th was held in Cashmere under the patronage of Kanishka (q.v.), probably about 70 A.D. Three commentaries were compiled. Although the Mahayana was not in existence as a specific school, its doctrines were promulgated at this Council, and the Hinayana School do not recognize it. The 5th was definitely Mahayana. It took place in 634 A.D. at Prayaga (Central India) under patronage of Siladitya. Here the doctrines of the Hinayana were condemned. The last Council took place at Madras in the year 1891. It was inaugurated by Colonel Olcott, Pres.-Founder of the Theosophical Society, in order to establish a statement of fundamental doctrine on which all sects and schools were agreed. The famous "Fourteen Fundamental Propositions" were drawn up and were accepted by representatives of both Hianyana and Mahayana Schools. v. *The Buddhist Catechism.* H. S. Olcott. Appendix.

CREATION: Buddhism has no conception of "creation" in the Western sense of a coming into existence from non-existence (*ex nihilo*). All existence is a beginningless and endless process of "becoming," subject to the law of causality (q.v.), but as all "*dhammas*" (v. *dhamma* [d]) are mind-created (*Dhp.* I, 1), the state of becoming depends on the mental development of the entity. All entities are "creatures," but are also "creators" of themselves and of their environment, to a greater or lesser extent according to their mental development. As beings progress in mental power, so have they greater freedom to create as they will, and the purer (more enlightened) the mind, the nearer the approach to the ideality of pure form.

DAGOBA: The *dagoba, tope,* or *stupa,* was a mound of earth or brick in which the bodies or ashes of important persons were deposited. In simple form they were pre-Buddhist, but by Buddhist times had become elaborate structures. The *stupa* discovered at Piprawa (accepted by some authorities as one of the original eight [or ten] erected over the relics of the Buddha), is estimated to have been "about the height of the dome of St. Paul's Cathedral, measured from the roof." (See Rh. D. *Buddhist India,* p. 83). The name *stupa* was usually reserved for those containing relics of the Buddha or of Arahats, otherwise they were called *dagobas.* The word *dagoba* is a contraction of *dhatugabbha* (relic cavity), and is more correctly spelled *dagaba.* (v. *Piprawa, Relics.*)

DANA (Sk & P): The virtue of alms-giving to the poor and needy; also, making gifts to a bhikkhu or community of bhikkhus. One of the three "acts of merit," *dana,* benevolence: *sila,* moral conduct: *bhavana,* meditation. The first of the 10 Paramitas. *Dana* in Bsm takes the place of sacrificial rites in Hinduism.

DEATH (P. *marana*): Is the temporary cessation of personal existence on the grosser material planes. It is only a temporary break in the continuous life of the individuality; an aspect of the impermanence (*anicca*) of all living things. The period between death and rebirth is spent in the super-physical, but still material spheres, which are the subjective worlds (*lokas*) created by the subconscious mind. (See *Bardo, Life.*)

DELUSION (P. *moha*): Is one of the three (or four) main blemishes of character, which must be eliminated before enlightenment is possible. The three are: *raga,* sensuality; *dosa,* ill-will; *moha,* delusion. *Lobha,* greed, is often included as a fourth. Moha may be defined as infatuation of the mind by erroneous ideas based on the illusion of "self."

DEPENDENT ORIGINATION (P. *Paticca Samuppada*): The Chain of phenomenal Cause and Effect by which birth and rebirth occur. (v. *Nidanas.*)

DESIRE (P. *tanha*): Thirst for separate existence in the worlds of sense. "Desire" in itself is colourless, but selfish desire is the cause of suffering. The "will to live" must be transmuted into "aspiration" for the welfare and ultimate enlightenment of all beings. (See *W.B.*, 57). *Tanha* is one of the twelve links in the chain of Causation (*Nidanas*), coming between *vedana* and *upadana*. Its source is delusion (*moha*) caused by attraction to the six objects of sense.

DEVA (Sk "*Shining One*"): Celestial beings, good, bad, or indifferent in nature. The devas inhabit the three world (v. *triloka*). They correspond to the angelic powers of Western theology.

DEVACHAN (Sk): "Dwelling place of shining ones," is the subjective state in which an individual lives between two earth "lives," after the death of the gross physical bodies and the separation of the *kama-rupa*. Such are usually termed "*devaputtas*" (sons of devas) in the Buddhist scriptures. There is much information on *devas* in *Dig. N.* (v. *Dial III Index.*) (v. *Sukhavati.*)

DEVIL: There are numerous classes of demons mentioned in the Buddhist scriptures. The personification of evil and the tempter of man is usually called Mara. The allegory of the Buddha's temptation by Mara is related in the *Mahavagga* (APC. 270*b*). *S.B.E.* X, p. 68. (See also *Mahavastu* ii 198 and *Lalitavistara* 329.) (v. *Evil.*)

DHAMMA (P.), DHARMA (Sk): The Pali form is generally used by the H. School, the Sanskrit by the M. School. Dharma, in sense of "the course of conduct right for a man at his particular stage of evolution," is now well known in the West, through its use in Theosophical literature.

Dhamma is one of the most difficult Buddhist technical terms to define. It comes from the Aryan root "*dhar,*" to uphold, sustain, support, and has been rendered into English by: system or doctrine, religion, virtue, moral quality, righteousness, duty, law, justice, standard, norm, ideal, truth, form, condition, cause, phenomenon, thing, cosmic order, and it may mean any of these according to the context. We may trace its basic meaning in the Latin *forma,* and Eng. *form*: that which supports, that which gives state or condition to the orderly arrangement of parts which makes a thing what it is; from which comes Eng. "good form": conduct appropriate to any given occasion.

Technical definitions come under five headings: A=Doctrine; B=Right; C=Condition; D=Phenomenon; E=Reality.

(A) *Dhamma*=Doctrine. Any teaching set forth as a formulated system; the guiding principles accepted or followed by a man; his religion. As pplied to Bsm: the Teachings of the Buddha. (See *Buddhism.*) Buddhists apply the meaning "Truth" also to the word as used in this connection, the *Buddha Dhamma* being regarded as synonymous with Truth.

(B) Right, Righteous conduct or righteousness, Law, Justice.

(C) Condition. Cause or causal antecedent. Cause and effect being practically identical, *dhamma* is here viewed from its causal side as in (d) it is viewed from aspect of effect.

(D) Phenomenon. Dhamma as effect. It is used in this sense in first verse of Dhp.: "all *dhammas* (phenomena) are mind created"; and in the famous formula *sabbe dhamma anicca, dukkha, anatta*—the whole of the phenomenal world is anicca, etc.

Application of word *dhamma* to phenomena indicates orderly nature of existence; universe is expression of Law.

(E) Ultimate Reality. In Mahayana *dharma* is synonymous with *Tathata* or Ultimate Reality. Cp. Suzuki in *A.F.M.*, p. 47, in which he says that he has been compelled to translate *dharma* as form, that which is possessed of form = a thing, law, truth, doctrine, and *Ultimate Reality*.

There is no other word in the P or Sk languages which so completely expresses the significant fact of the basic unity of all life as this word *dhamma*.

Dharmas:—Nine Mahayana scriptures considered of supreme importance as containing complete exposition of exoteric and esoteric teachings of Buddha. Called the *Vaipulya Sutras*, they comprise: *Ashtasahasrika Prajñaparamita*: *Ganda-vyuha*: *Dasabhumisvara*: *Samadhi-raja*: *Lankavatara Sutra*: *Saddharma-Pundarika*: *Tathagata-guhyaka*: *Lalita-vistara*: *Suvarna-prabhasa*. (Nos. 5 and 6 available in English, 8 in French.)

DHAMMACAKKAPPAVATTANA SUTTA: The setting in motion of the Wheel of the Good Law, or Sutra of the Foundation of the Kingdom of Righteousness. The first discourse of the Buddha after His Enlightenment. Delivered to his first converts in the Deer Park at Benares. (See *B.E. I.*, p. 61, and *Selected Buddhist Scriptures* (B. Lodge Pamphlets, No. 2).

DHAMMAPADA: Law Verses. Canonical Pali Scripture. English versions by M. Müller, Woodward, Saunders, Beal, Edmunds, Bhagwat, and see condensed version in "*Selected Buddhist Scriptures*" (B. Lodge Pamphlet, No. 2).

DHAMMAPALA: Sri Devamitta Dhammapala was the name taken by the Anagarika Dharmapala (q.v.) on entering the Sangha, July 13th, 1931.

DHAMMA-SANGANI: The first part of the Abhidhamma Pitaka. Eng. trsl. *Buddhist Manual of Psychological Ethics* (P.T.S.).

DHARMAKAYA: The Body of the Law. The Buddha as the personification of Truth. In Mahayana one of the triple aspects of Bhutatathata. The Essence Body: "Consciousness merged in the Universal Consciousness." (See *W.B.*, p. 170.)

DHYANA (Sk), *Jhana* (P), (Chin. *Ch'an*; Jap. *Zen*): Mystic states of serene contemplation attained by meditation. *Jhana* is one of the six Paramitas of Perfection. Six states are recognized, but only in the highest is utter elimination of idea of "self" attained, and the complete union with Reality (*Samadhi*) experienced. These mystic states are not an end in themselves, but only means to attainment of *Jhanavimokkha*, i.e., emancipation through *Jhana*. (v. *Samadhi, Zen.*)

DHYANI BUDDHAS: The personifications of the seven creative aspects or modes of manifestation of the primordial Adi-Buddha (called also *Vishvarupa*, "that principle which is eternally manifest in infinite forms"). These are the "creators" of the phenomenal universe, the first five being concerned with the worlds of form, the last two, with the "formless" worlds. (v. *Rupa.*) The names of the first five are: *Vairochana, Akshobhya, Ratna-Sambhava, Amitabha, Amoghasiddha*. The name of the sixth is *Vajrasattva*. No name has been given to the seventh. In Tibet the Dhyani Buddhas are called "Jinas" (victors). An exceedingly complicated pantheon of deities is evolved from the Dhyani Buddhas, for details of which see Waddell, *Buddhism of Tibet*.

DIGHA NIKAYA: The "Collection of Long Discourses" is the first section of the *Sutta Pitaka* (q.v.). For analysis see *APC*. 3-4, and for trsls., p. 16. *Dialogues of the Buddha*, vols. I-III contain whole of Digha.

DOSA (P): Depravity of mind due to anger, ill-will, hatred. One of the three (or four) cardinal blemishes of the character. (v. *raga, moha, lobha.*)

DUGPA: A sub-sect of the Kar-gyu sect founded by Marpa (q.v.) in Tibet. It was founded by Pag-

Sam-Wangpo in the 12th c. at Ralung Monastery, near Gyan-tse. The term is often applied (erroneously, according to Waddell) to all the Red Cap sects. The word dugpa is now synonymous with "sorcerer," its teaching being a mixture of Bön sorcery and degraded Tantricism.

DUKKHA (P), DUHKHA (*duhka*) (Sk): Ordinarily translated as "suffering or ill." The P.D., however, states that "there is no word in English covering the same ground as *dukkha* does in Pali." Ordinarily set in opposition to *sukha* ease and well-being, it signifies dis-ease in the sense of discomfort, and ill-being or disharmony with environment.

In its philosophic form, as used in the Pali Scriptures in describing the characteristics and limitations of existence it signifies every form of discomfort and ill experienced with the breaking up of form. It can best be described by the colloquial expression, "growing pains."

The assertion that life is Suffering is one of the Four Noble Truths. Every phase of existence is characterized by *dukkha,* said the Buddha. This description may appear a somewhat exaggerated one at first sight, but due consideration will show that suffering, in a greater or lesser degree, from mere disharmony to extreme agony of mind or body, is naturally associated with every effort to adapt oneself to that ever-changing environment which is the outcome of the "will to live."

Dukkha is included in the Three Characteristics of Existence, with *anicca,* impermanence, and *anatta,* unreality, *dukkha* being the effect of *anicca* and *anatta.* It follows, therefore, that existence cannot be wholly separated from *dukkha,* and that complete escape from it is possible only by liberation from the round of birth and death.

Dukkha is the last link in the Chain of Dependent Origination, *Jaramarana,* old age and death, being characterized as inseparable from *soka pari-*

deva dukkha domanass' upayâsâ (grief, lamentation, sorrow, distress and despair).

"EASTERN BUDDHIST": The Journal of The Eastern Buddhist Society, Otani Daigaku, Kyoto, Japan. Published one or more times a year at irregular intervals. Editors: D. T. Suzuki and B. L. Suzuki, 61, Higashi Onocho, Koyama, Kyoto, Japan. Sub., six yen each four issues.

EDUCATION: Enlightenment on every plane of existence being the Buddhist goal, education naturally plays an important part in the Buddhist scheme of life. Ignorance can be removed, and truth attained only by experience, and experience must be obtained from life; an understanding of life is therefore essential. Bsm therefore encourages science, arts and crafts, and its influence has always been for the elevation of the people. Buddhist "education" emphasizes the development of innate faculties by self-control, not mere acquirement of facts concerning the phenomenal world. Knowledge of the physical world is encouraged, however, as helping to discourage superstitious beliefs regarding the nature of life. The Buddhist monastery is often a school, and Buddhist countries are noted for the literacy of the people. The last census report of Burma, for example, gave 95 per cent. of the male population as literate. In Japan, Bsm introduced and fostered art and science, and built up the national culture. (v. *Anuradhapura, Nalanda.*)

EGO: Bsm denies an ego in the sense of a self in man ultimately separate from the self in every other man. The belief in an ego creates and fosters egoism and desire, thus preventing the realization of the unity of life and the attainment of enlightenment. (v. *Anatta.*)

EIGHTFOLD NOBLE PATH: The Bst scheme of moral and intellectual self-development leading to Enlightenment. The eight constituent parts are:

(1) *Sammâ Ditthi,* Right Understanding or views; (2) *Sammâ Sankappo,* Right Mental Attitude or Motive; (3) *Sammâ Vacha,* Right Speech or expression of one's thoughts; (4) *Sammâ Kammanto,* Right Action; (5) *Sammâ Ajivo,* Right Pursuits, including means of Livelihood and employment of Leisure; (6) *Sammâ Vayamo,* Right Mindfulness; (7) *Sammâ Sati,* Right Concentration of Mind; (8) *Sammâ Samadhi,* Right Ecstasy, or Spiritual Contemplation of Reality. (v. *Sammâ.*)

ESOTERIC: (1) Secret; in the sense of teaching not revealed to those unworthy or unfit to receive it. Such teaching may refer to phenomenal or spiritual matters. (2) Symbolic; the inner or spiritual meaning underlying the literal surface meaning. Spiritual truths are apprehended by the intuition (v. *bodhi*) and cannot be revealed or explained, except to those whose inner development enables them to grasp them. The "Heart" doctrine, as opposed to the "Eye" doctrine.

Esoteric teaching is not contrary to exoteric, but is a spiritual and therefore truer interpretation of it. In other words, exoteric doctrine is an effort to express spiritual truths in a form capable of being grasped by the intellect and so awakening the intuition.

The Esoteric Schools in Bsm base their teaching on the higher truths revealed by the Buddha to his disciples who were ready to receive it. Nagarjuna, the Apostle of Buddhist mysticism, tells us that every Buddha has both a revealed and a mystic doctrine. The former is set forth in the *Suttas*; the latter cannot be expressed in words, but must be apprehended by the faculty of *buddhi* latent in the heart of every man.

The statement attributed to the Buddha, denying that he taught an esoteric doctrine, appears in *Sam. N.* (see "Kindred Sayings," Vol. v, p. 132.)

ETHICS: Buddhist ethics are based on the doctrine of *Anatta* (q.v.), therefore, every quality encouraging altruism is considered a virtue, and every opposite quality a vice. The Buddhist moral code is set forth in the Noble Eightfold Path and in the Five Precepts (v. *Buddhism, Pansil*). The standard work on Buddhist ethics is *The Ethics of Buddhism*, by S. Tachibana (London, 1926), 15/-. (See also *Buddha's Golden Path*, Goddard, 1930.)

EVIL: Bsm is not dualistic, and therefore does not divide phenomena into absolute "good" or "evil." It recognizes "evil" as "limitation," and therefore purely relative. There is therefore no "problem of Evil" as in theistic systems of thought. All evil is traced to desire (v. *tanha*) for self. The "basic evil" is the idea of separateness, and the Buddhist goal is the removal of evil by the eradication of every selfish inclination.

EVOLUTION: The principle of "origination from antecedent causes" (v. *Nidanas*) rules the Buddhist conception of existence, periods of involution and evolution eternally succeeding one another. These are described in the English translations of the scriptures as periods of evolution and disintegration, but the latter term must not be understood as passing into nothingness for Bsm recognizes no coming into existence from nothingness nor passing away into nothingness. For example, see *Dig. N. i*, 17. (*Dial, i, p*, 30.) The principle underlying the modern theories of evolution is therefore accepted, only that evolution is conceived of as an unfolding (*e-voluo*) or expression of potential powers inherent in life. Evolution may be defined, therefore, as the unfolding of Life and its more and more perfect expression in form, taking place under inviolable Law.

EXISTENCE (*Ex-isto*): Coming out of Being. The "becoming" under the limitations of time, space and causation, of that infinite One Life which in its essence transcends all limitation. (v. *Life, Evolution, Tathata.*)

FAITH: Faith in Bsm does not imply mental acceptance of doctrinal beliefs, it signifies confidence in the Teacher and the Doctrine, with consequent effort to live according to their example and precept.

Some writers (see *Compendium, pp.* 283-5) have asserted that a Buddhist follows authority and accepts his religion on faith. This is an erroneous and wholly misleading assertion. (v. *Authority.*)

Faith, in the sense of reliance on the authority of another is entirely absent from Buddhism. The Buddha in his admonition to the Kalamans (*Ang. N.* III, 65) enjoins freedom of thought, and acceptance of his teaching only after subjecting it to the searching test of reason and experience.

In the Mahayana, Faith means reliance on the Buddha within (Amitabha, the Higher Self), and the practice of the highest virtues. (v. *Asvaghosa. Paramitas.*)

FETTERS: The Ten Fetters are certain erroneous mental conceptions and desires which have to be cast off as the Path is followed to the Goal. These are enumerated under the heading Four Paths (q.v.) *Fetter*: A "Fetter" is the meaning of the name of the Buddha's son, Rahula.

FLESH FOOD is discouraged as breaking the rule of ahimsa set forth in the first of the Five Precepts. (v. *Pansil.*) Certain rules are set forth under which flesh food is permitted, but its entire non-use is recommended. The rules are: He who eats must not kill the animal himself, nor order or permit another to kill it for him. He must have no knowledge that the animal was killed: i.e., he may assume it died a natural death. In Tibet, the earnest Buddhist abstains from flesh on the 8th, 15th and 30th days of the month, and during the whole of the first month of the year.

Abstinence from meat is recommended as tending to assist control over sensual desires. As the psychic centres unfold with the development of the *iddhi* (q.v.) powers, elimination of all flesh food becomes essential. For M. viewpoint see *Studies in Lankavatara S.*, pp. 368 sqq.

FOUR NOBLE TRUTHS: The basic truths of Bsm, as set forth by the Buddha in his first Sermon. They are: *Dukkha*: There can be no existence without "suffering"; *Samudaya*: The cause of Suffering is egoistic Desire (tanha); *Nirodha*: The elimination of Desire brings the cessation of Suffering; *Marga*: The Way to the elimination of Desire is the Noble Eightfold Path (q.v.).

FOUR PATHS: The Four Paths or Stages on the Path to liberation are (I) SOTAPANNA: "He who has entered the Stream." At this stage he is free from the first three of the Ten Fetters (*saññojanas*), i.e., *Sakkaya-ditthi*; the illusion of being a "self" separate from all other selves. (2) *Vicikiccha*; mental vacillation, doubt. (3) *Silabbata-paramasa*; belief in the efficacy of Rites and Ceremonies.

The second stage is (II) SAKADAGAMIN: "He who will return once only" to this world before attaining liberation. Such is free from (4) *Kâmacchando*, delusions of the senses. (5) *Patigha* or *Vyapado*; ill-will or aversion.

(III) ANAGAMIN: "He who will never return" to this world. He is free from (6) *Ruparaga*; desire for existence in the worlds of form (the gross and subtle sense worlds), (7) *Aruparaga*; desire for existence in the formless worlds (the higher heaven worlds).

(IV) ARAHAT: "The Worthy One." He who attains Nirvana at the death of his present body. Such has cast off the last three Fetters (8) *Mâno*, self-esteem, and (9) *Uddhaccam*, self-righteousness, and (10) *Avijja*, ignorance.

FOURTEEN FUNDAMENTAL BUDDHIST BELIEFS: The Fourteen Points compiled at the Council organized by Col. H. S. Olcott at Adyar, Madras, India, 8th to 12th January, 1891, A.D.

(2434 B.E.), and accepted by the representatives of Burma, Ceylon, Japan (nine sects), and Chittagong; and later by the Chief Mongolian lamas. The points are set forth in the Appendix to Olcott's *Buddhist Catechism*, pp. 111-118.

FREEWILL: Determinism, in the sense that human action is determined by forces independent of the will, is classed in Bsm as an erroneous conception. It asserts that the will of man is not bound by external causes, but is free in the sense that all the fetters which bind it are of man's own making, and may be cast off in so far as he disregards his own interests and considers those of others. In other words: will *per se* is free, but is limited to a greater or lesser degree by the form it energizes, which form (the Five Skandhas) is the creation of the individual himself.

Karma (action and the result of action) frees or binds according as it is or is not free from the poison of *tanha*.

In the *Ang. N.* the Buddha has expressed this non-deterministic view thus: "If anyone asserts, O Bhikkhus, that a man must reap according to his deeds, in that case there is no religious life, nor is any opportunity afforded for the entire extinction of ill. But if anyone says that the reward a man reaps accords with his deeds, in that case, O Bhikkhus, there is a religious life, and opportunity is afforded for the entire extinction of ill." Here we have the declaration that the Law pre-destines no one, the abolition of the false antithesis of freedom to Law, and the recognition that utter reliance on the Law will create the conditions which will release the personality from the fetters of "self" and bring unconditioned freedom. (v. *W.B.*, p. 127.)

GANDHARA: The Sk name for the district now called Peshawar in British India. After great vicissitudes of fortune it became a Buddhist stronghold

(3rd c. A.D.) and played an important part in the evolution of the doctrines of the Mahayana School. It is famous for its peculiar style of sculpture which is a blend of ancient Indian modified by Alexandrian influence (as exemplified by Bharut, Sanchi, etc.), and that of the Græco-Roman styles of Asia Minor. Its period was 100-300 A.D. Ancient Indian Buddhist art did not depict the figure of the Buddha but symbolized his presence; Gandhara art always depicts the figure, the whole life history of the Buddha being drawn upon for scenes. The sculpture of Amaravati represents an intermediate stage, both symbol and figure being used. The Gandhara period was a decadent stage in Indian art, and it made no permanent impression on Indian ideals. The best work on Gandhara art is Fourcher, *L'Art Bouddhique du Gandhara* (1905). (See also E. B. Havell, *Ideals of Indian Art*. Murray (1911).)

GAYA: Buddha Gaya. The place where the Buddha attained Enlightenment. It is situated about six miles to the south of the town of Gaya (24 N. 85 E.) the site being marked by the Maha-Bodhi Temple and the famous Bodhi Tree under which the Blessed One sat.

GOD: Bsm does not personify Ultimate Reality, nor does it teach reliance on an external deity. Man is innately divine, and must rely upon his own efforts to attain complete realization of that divinity, which is "Enlightenment." The forces of nature or natural laws personified as gods or devas, are not petitioned or worshipped. The theistic sects of the Mahayana School (v. *Adi-Buddha*) deify these cosmic principles, and the "Pure Land" sects personify and worship the "Higher Self" of man under the name *Amitabha*. These are recognized as *upâyas* or methods of expediency, however, and do not constitute dogmas. The Mahayana School generally recognizes the Ultimate Reality or substantial essence of the universe as *Tathata* (essence of Being) but does not personify or worship this

Principle, other than by striving to attain harmony with it. (v. *Atheism. Tathata.*)

GOTAMA (P), GAUTAMA (Sk): The gotra or clan name of the Buddha. It is a Brahmin name, although the clan was a Kshattriya one. There was a famous Hindu philosopher of the same name who lived about 150 B.C. and founded the Nyâya system, the latest of the six orthodox philosophical schools.

HAWAII: A number of islands in the Pacific forming a political sub-division of the U.S.A. Capital city Honolulu, on the island of Oahu. Pop. 350,000, of whom about 80,000 are Buddhist. Bsm started with the establishment of the Honpa Hongwanji Mission in 1897, which was founded for the Japanese immigrants. In 1927 an English Language Section was formed. This movement follows the doctrines of Shin-shu (q.v.). There are also Zen, Jodo, Shingon and Nichiren sects established in the islands.

See *Buddhism in Hawaii,* Hongwanji Buddhist Mission, Honolulu (1929, 66 pp. 1/- p.f.).

HEART: The word "heart" is used in P. and Sk. to indicate the higher emotions as it is in European languages. It is (figuratively) *Buddhi* or the seat of the divine intuition, the reflection of *Bodhi* in the mind. "Our hearts are the seat of the Buddha nature," says a Buddhist mystic. The "heart doctrine" is the inner or spiritual interpretation of the *dhamma,* as opposed to the literal, or outer "eye doctrine."

HEAVEN: (v. *Devachan. Sukhavati.*)

HELL: There is no hell in the sense of a state of endless torture known to Bsm. The various hells are purgatorial states called *apayas,* these including the nirayas, the animal world, the ghost or peta world, the demon or asura world. Avichi (*avicimahaniraya*) is the lowest and most severe of the *apaya* states. One school teaches that in this state all attributes of humanity are lost and the entity is annihilated, another, that release into the higher purgatorial regions eventually comes. (See *Tibetan Book of the Dead, Mahatma Letters, Petta-vatthu.*)

HINAYANA: The name given to the school of Buddhism which developed from the primitive or Theravada (q.v.). By the time of King Milinda (see *Q.K.M.*), c. 100 B.C., there were 18 Hinayana sects (v. *B.E.* iv, p. 204). The term "Hinayana" means Lesser Vehicle (of salvation) and was coined originally by Mahayana followers as a term of reproach, but is now used as a convenient word to designate the school which adheres to the doctrine as expounded in the Pali Canon. The H. School is also known as the "Southern School." Geographically, it includes Ceylon, Burma, Siam, and Cambodia. (v. *India. Mahayana. Theravada.*)

HONEN: Honen Shonin or Genku (1133-1211) was the founder of the Jodo-Shu or "Pure Land Sect" in Japan. Standard life is: *Honen, His Life and Teaching*, Coates and Ishizuka. Kyoto (1925). 40/-. (v. *Jodo. Pure Land.*)

HONGWANJI (*or Honganji*). The head temples of the two most important sections of the Jodo-Shinshu are called Nishi Hongwanji (Western H.), and Higashi Hongwanji (Eastern H.) respectively. The former was founded by Kakushin, the youngest daughter of Shinran Shonin, and the latter by Kyônyo, in 1602.

IDDHIS (Sk *Siddhi, riddhi*): Attributes or powers of a state (of perfection). There are ten iddhis or supernormal powers developed in following the path to arahatship: these include clairvoyance, clairaudience, telepathy, recalling one's former lives and those of others, etc. It is forbidden to use these psychic powers (the lower *iddhis*) for one's personal benefit. The higher *iddhis* are the spiritual Modes of Mystic Insight attained by the practice of *dhyana* (q.v.).

INDIA: Bsm founded in India by Gautama Buddha, c. 500 B.C. Adopted by Asoka as state religion of his empire, c. 250 B.C. (v. *Asoka*). Flourished under the kings Milanda (c. 100 B.C.), Kanishka (c. 80 A.D.) and Harsha (606-648 A.D.): the two latter converts to the Mahayana School. Declined after Muhammedan conquest of Sindh 712 A.D., and finally suppressed by Muhammedan persecution 1200 A.D. Max Müller predicted a revival of Bsm in India, and there are indications that this may be fulfilled. (See Pratt *Pilgrimage of Bsm*. Rh. D. *Hibbert Lectures*, 1881. *B.E.*, vol. iii, 156. iv, 87, 203.)

INDIVIDUALITY: That aspect of consciousness (*viññana*) which is the permanent link between all phenomenal states of consciousness: the sub-consciousness in which is stored all the experiences of the past, as distinct from the personality which is the temporary expression of certain of these sub-conscious characteristics. (v. *Mano Viññana*.)

ITI-VUTTAKA: One of the books of the *Khu. N.* (*APÇ.* 266). A collection of 112 short suttas. It takes its name from the words introducing each set of verses—*iti vuccati*, "thus it is said." The teaching is mainly ethical.

JAPAN: Bsm entered Japan (c. 550 A.D.) from Korea, then consisting of several small independent kingdoms. The Empress Suiko became a convert, and also the Prince Regent Umayado (better known as Shotoku Taishi), who, recognizing the high ethical teaching and profound philosophy of Bsm, did all in his power to encourage it. He drew up Japan's first "Constitution," proclaiming the "Triune Treasure": the Buddha, the Dhamma, the Sangha, as the basis of the national life, and devotion to it the fundamental factor of a noble life. He built temples, schools and hospitals, and asylums for the aged and infirm. From that time Japan entered upon a new phase of history, gradually taking over and making her own the fruit of centuries of Chinese culture. In the next 70 years, a number of sects were established, and Nara became the religious and secular capital. In the ninth century, Dengyo Daishi, the founder of the Tendai Sect, and Kobo Daishi, the founder of the Shingon Sect, harmonized Buddhism with Shinto, producing the Ryobu Shinto (two-sided Shinto), a fusion which lasted for a thousand years.

About the year 1100, Ryonin founded the Yudzu Nembutsu, the first of the Amida sects, and the first distinctively Japanese. Thirty years later Honen brought the Jodo Sect from China, from which developed the Shin Sect, founded by Shinran. The small Ji Sect makes up the four main "Pure Land" sects of Japan.

The Zen and Nichiren Sects were founded by adherents of the Tendai, who established independent sects of their own; the former by Eisai (c. 1200 A.D.), who studied Zen doctrine in China; the latter by Nichiren in 1253, who based his doctrine on the *Saddharma Pundarika*, the only scripture he considered worth studying.

Biblio: *Japanese Bsm.* Sir Chas. Eliot, London (1935). *The Creed of Half Japan,* Lloyd. London (1911). *History of Japanese Religion.* *Anesaki.* London (1930).

JATAKA: a birth story. A book of the *Khu. N.* (*APC.* 277), containing 550 stories purporting to be accounts of former lives of the Buddha. For English transl. see *APC.*, p. 18.

JATI (P): Birth, and disposition towards re-birth. The 11th link in the Chain of Causation. The coming into existence as the result of previous karma. Re-birth into the physical world as a personality, the outcome of the karma of past personalities.

JIRIKI (Jap): Salvation through one's own efforts, as opposed to "Tariki," salvation through the efforts of another. All Japanese sects are divided into these two divisions. Jodo, for example, is a *Tariki* sect, Nichiren a *Jiriki*. (v. *Tariki*.)

JIZO: The Japanese name of the pusa or bodhisattva known in China as Ti-tsang. His special care are the spirits in the various hells, whom he visits and encourages. He is also the patron saint of young children. (See Johnston, *Buddhist China*, and Hearn, *Glimpses of Unfamiliar Japan*.)

JOSAPHAT (corruption of Bodhisat; also corrupted into Yosaphat and Yudasaf): The account of the canonization of the Buddha by the Roman and Greek sects of Christianity is related in the story of Barlaam and Josaphat. The best brief account is "*How the Buddha became a Christian Saint*," Will Hayes, 24 pp., 6d. For Biblio., see *Buddhist Birth Stories*, Mrs. Rh. D., pp. 239-242. In the Greek Church, August 26th is dedicated to St. Josaphat, and in the R.C., November 27th is dedicated to both Barlaam and Josaphat.

KAMA (Sk): Desire of the senses, especially sexual desire. Kâma is one of the four *asavas*, and is the first of the six factors of existence, the elimination of which is essential for liberation from rebirth. The six are *kâma, vedanâ, saññâ, âsavâs, kamma, dukkha*. The kâma-lokas are the worlds of sense desire or purgatorial after-death states. Kâma must not be confused with *kamma* (q.v.).

KANISHKA: An Indo-Scythian king who was instrumental in spreading Mahayana Bsm in India and Afghanistan (c. 80 A.D.). He was a convert to Bsm of M. School and convened the great council at Purusapura (Peshawar) at which Asvaghosha confounded the adherents of the Hinayana doctrines. His powerful patronage spread Bsm all over India, and as far east at Chinese Turkestan.

KAPILAVATTHU: The birthplace of the Buddha. Modern Piprâwâ in the Nepal Tarai, approx. 83 E., 27½ N. The actual birthplace of Lumbini is about 15 miles to the S.E. (v. *Rummindei*). The famous Piprawa stupa discovered by W. C. Peppé in 1898 *may* be one of the original stupas erected over the relics of the Buddha after his death. (v. *Piprawa.*)

KARMA (Sk): Pali *kamma*. Root, meaning "action"; derived meaning, "action and the appropriate result of action"; the law of cause and effect. Karma operates on all planes of existence. As applied to the moral sphere it is the Law of Ethical Causation, through the operation of which a man "reaps what he sows," builds his character, makes his destiny, and works out his salvation.

Karma is not limited by time or space, and is not strictly individual; there is group karma, family, national, etc. (See *W.B.*, pp. 67 and 90.)

The doctrine of re-birth is an essential corollary to that of karma, the individual coming into physical life with a character and into an environment resulting from his actions in the past. His character and destiny are, therefore, popularly (and correctly) called his "karma," and according to his reaction to his present destiny he modifies and builds his future. Karma (action) in itself does not bind to the wheel of re-birth; it is personal desire for the fruit of action that binds. Liberation is therefore achieved by elimination of desire for self. (v. *tanhâ, re-birth.*)

KARUNA (Sk): Active pity or compassion. One of the Four *Brahma Viharas* or Divine States resulting from the elimination of selfish inclinations. (v. *W.B.*, 140.)

KATHA VATTHU: The fifth of the seven works composing the Abhidhamma Pitaka. It deals with matters of controversy between the eighteen Hinayana sects. Eng. trsl. *Points of Controversy or Subjects of Discourse.* S. Z. Aung and Mrs. R. H. D. (P.T.S.) 1915.

KLESA (KILESA) (Sk): Moral depravity or inclination to vice, the elimination of which as *raga, dosa, moha,* is essential to progress on the Path.

KOAN (Jap): In Zen Buddhism the kôans are problems couched in unfamiliar and often seemingly non-sensical form, which are given the student as subjects for meditation. They are means of developing the intuition rather than intellectual problems. There are famous *koans* still used which have been handed down since the time of the Zen Patriarchs, from Bodhidharma downwards. (v. *B.E.*, iii, 187, and v. 176.) (v. *Za-zen. Zen.*)

KOREA: Bsm was introduced from one of the smaller Chinese kingdoms between 350-370 A.D., and by about 500 A.D. had become the state religion. Under its influence Korea attained a high state of prosperity and culture. Confucianism became state religion under new dynasty about 1500 A.D. Revival of Bsm started about 50 years ago, and mass of the people now Buddhist. *Korean Buddhism,* Starr; Boston (1918). *Korea and her neighbours,* Bishop. *Korean Beliefs,* Gale; Yokohama (1897).

KOSALA: The ruling clan in the Kingdom of Kosala at the time of the Buddha, in that part of N. India corresponding to modern Nepal. The capital city was Savatthi, where the Buddha spent much of his time, and Benares was in the same kingdom. The Kingdom of K. was the paramount power in N. India from 7th c. B.C. until its absorption into that of Magadha, c. 300 B.C. The language known to us as Pali was the official form of Prakrit written and spoken at the court at Savatthi.

KSHATTRIYA: At the time of the Buddha the Aryan clans in India recognized four social grades called *vannas* (Sk *varna,* a colour), the highest being the Kshattriya or warrior-statesmen, next the Brahmin or priest, after which came the common people, the Vessas or Vaishyas, and lastly the Sudras or people of non-Aryan descent. Members of each caste did not necessarily follow the actual profession assigned to it, and the lines of demarcation between each *vanna* were variable and undefined: the complexity and rigidity of the modern caste system was unknown. The Buddha belonged to the *kshattriya vanna.*

KUSINAGARA (KUSINARA): The "little wattle-and-daub township in the midst of the jungle" where the Buddha passed into parinibbana. One of the Four Holy Places of Bsm. It is usually identified with Kasia 26.45 N. 83.55 E., but V. Smith prefers to place it at the confluence of the Little Rapti and Gandak rivers in Nepal.

KWANNON (Jap), KWAN-YIN (Chin): The feminine aspect of the Bodhisattva Avalokitesvara; worshipped in China and Japan as the incarnation of divine compassion, the "*pusa* of a thousand hands and a thousand eyes," ever working to relieve the sorrows of mankind. (See Broughton: *Vision of Kwannon Sama* (1929).)

LALITA VISTARA: A biography of the Buddha written in Sanskrit. Originally compiled by Hinayana School, it has been added to by Mahayana writers, and now demonstrates development of the legendary elements in his life. One of the nine Vaipulya Sutras (v. *dharma*). No Eng. translation, but one in French, Foucaux (1884-92). The *Life of the Buddha,* by N. J. Krom, consists of matter translated from the Lalita Vistara, and Arnold's *Light of Asia* is based on it. (See also *Bsm* (S.P.C.K.), p. 11.)

LAMA: Correctly applied only to the higher orders of the religious hierarchy of Tibet, the word is now used to designate any monk: Gelong is correct name for ordinary monk. The head lamas of the Church are: (1) The Tashi Lama (Panchen Rimpoche), who is the supreme spiritual head, and is considered to be an incarnation of Amitabha. (2) The Dalai Lama, who is concerned with the relationship of the Church and State, and as such is the temporal ruler. (3) The Bogdo Lama (Bogdo-Gegen), who lives at Urga in Mongolia, and who is the representative of both Tashi and Dalai Lamas for the Mongolian Buddhists outside Tibet.

LANKAVATARA SUTRA: One of the Vaipulva Sutras or Dharmas of Mahayana. One of the most important M. works, as it includes all the essential M. tenets, and is the one work accepted by the Zen sect as expounding its basic principles. Trans. D. T. Suzuki, London, 1932. His *Studies in the Lankavatara Sutra* is the best introduction.

LIFE: The Buddhist takes life as it is, neither postulating its beginning nor conceiving its end. It has two aspects relative, as existence, a state of becoming; and absolute, as Being (or Be-ness), the fount or source of becoming.

In brief, Life is One: a monistic or indivisible unity which expresses or manifests itself in a diversity of forms. The Buddhist aims at realizing this innate unity of life in his every thought and action in order to expand his consciousness to that point where it will blend with the One Life and become perfected.

Taking of Life. The first of the five Precepts enjoins abstinence from taking life, or more correctly from breaking up the form through which the life is being expressed. Life after Death: (see *Bardo. Death. Existence. Jati.*)

LIGHT OF ASIA: Famous poetical work by Sir Edwin Arnold, first published in 1879. The Life and Teaching of the Buddha in verse. " A work of great beauty and intense interest." Editions from 1/- to 10/6.

LIVELIHOOD (*Samma Ajivo*): Right Livelihood is the Fifth Stage of the Noble Eightfold Path (q.v.).

The ignoble trades—those which a true Buddhist should avoid—include butchery, hunting and fishing, warfare and the making of weapons of war, dealing in poisons, drugs and drinks which cause stupefaction and intoxication, and dealing in the bodies of men and women, as slaves, prostitutes, etc.

LOBHA (P): Covetousness or greed; often added as a fourth to the three cardinal moral defects: *raga, dosa, moha.*

LOGOS: The idea of a personification of the Absolute as a creative deity is found only in certain sects of Mahayana Bsm. The primal Adi-Buddha is a trinity of creative activity, wisdom and love, which manifests through the seven rays of creative activity personified as the seven Dhyani Buddhas and their corresponding Bodhisattvas. (v. *Bhutatathata.*)

LOTUS: The symbol of divine perfection and purity. As the emblem of the Dhyani Buddhas it signifies the self-creative force of the cosmos, especially personified in the Dhyani Bodhisattva Avalokitesvara. Birth in the Paradise of Amitabha where sex differentiations are unknown, is likened to the Lotus springing into flower from the water. See Johnston *Bud. China*, p. 103. *Lotus of the True Law* = title of English trsl. of the *Saddharma Pundarika* (q.v.). v. AUM!

LOVE (*metta, karunâ*): Altruistic aspiration for the welfare of one's fellow-beings, is classed with wisdom as the two supreme virtues, the state of Buddhahood implying perfection in both. (See Frontispiece and Preface to Suzuki *A.F.M.*)

LUMBINI: The Buddha was born in the Lumbini Park, near Kapilavatthu. The spot is marked by a pillar placed there by King Asoka (c. 250 B.C.). This is called the Rummindei Pillar, from the village near (85 E. 26 N.).

LUST: v. *kâma*, sensual lust: *râga*, passion, lust for emotional excitement: *tanhâ*, lust of life: all obstacles to liberation.

MAGIC: In the sense of using ritual or mantric formula for obtaining material benefits is deprecated in Bsm. Belief in the efficacy of rites and ceremonies (as means of attaining liberation) is one of the Ten Fetters to be cast off in following the Path. (v. *Fetters.*)

MAHAPARINIRVANA SUTRA: A scripture of the M. School, called also the "Paradise Sutra." (Jap. *Nehankyo*): Teaches that all beings have the Buddha-nature innate in them, the unfoldment of which by the practice of the Paramitas constitutes Nirvana. Not to be confused with the *Mahaparinibbana Sutta* (*APC.* 16).

MAHASANGHIKAS: A school between the Hinayana and the Mahayana, but classed as Hinayana, showing a stage of development between the two. It taught a pantheistic interpretation of the *dhamma*, and the doctrine that the Buddha appeared on earth to teach it in an illlusory body, whilst dwelling in mystic contemplation in *nibbana*.

MAHAYANA: The School of the "Great Vehicle" of Salvation, also (incorrectly) called the "Northern School." Geographically it includes Tibet and Mongolia (Western Mahayana), and China, Japan, Korea and Hawaii (Eastern Mahayana), cp. *Hinayana*. The Mahayana gradually developed from the primitive teaching, and no sharp line of demarcation has ever existed; the doctrines of the Mahasanghika School (q.v.) contain all the basic elements of the developed Mahayana. *Teaching*: The teaching of the M. is more distinctly religious, making its appeal to the heart and not the mind, to the intuition rather than the intellect. It seeks the spiritual interpretation of the verbal teaching and endeavours to expound that teaching in a variety of forms calculated to appeal to every type of mind and every stage of spiritual development. For this reason it calls itself the Great or Universal Vehicle. Yet it fully recognizes that this method is but a concession to man's limitations; an accommodation of Truth to the intelligence of the hearer. This fact must be borne in mind when considering certain M. teachings, especially of the "Pure Land" School, which appear fundamentally opposed to the original teaching of the Buddha. Mahayana discountenance asceticism of any kind, its "Sangha" being a body of teachers rather than monks. It is (pan)theistic rather than atheistic. The Hinayana in so far as it recognizes a transcendental Reality at all, conceives of it as obscured or hidden by the phenomenal, whereas in M. the Eternal and Real is being ever revealed by the phenomenal. The Mahayanist therefore learns through life; the Hinayanist tries to escape from life. The Goal of the H. is the attainment of Arahatship, self-salvation; that of the M. is Bodhisattva-hood, renunciation of Nirvana in order to help humanity in its pilgrimage thereto. There is no complete work on M. development and doctrine. Dr. Suzuki's work (*Outlines M.B.*) is the best work extant. An introductory work is in preparation. Summaries are given in *B.E.* III, p. 4 and V. p. 15. See also Suzuki: *A.F.M.* Reichauer: *Japanese Bsm.* Anesaki: *History of Jap. Religion.* McGovern: *Intro. to M. Bsm.*

MAITREYA (Sk), METTEYA (P): The "Buddha of Compassion" who is to come in the far future, as foretold in the *Anagata Vamsa,* a non-canonical Pali work. The only reference to Metteya in the Canon is in the 26th Sutta of the Digha (*Dial.* III, p. 73) where the Buddha says: "There will arise an Exalted One named Metteya . . . who will teach the dhamma in its purity . . . whose followers will number thousands as mine number hundreds." (See Warren: *Bsm in Trsl.*, pp. 481-486.)

MAJJHIMA NIKAYA: The second of the five main divisions of the Sutta Pitaka. v. APC, pp. 3 and 16. Eng. trsl. *Further Dialogues of the Buddha*, 2 vols. (P.T.S.).

MANO (P), MANAS (Sk): Mind; the rational faculty in man. That aspect of consciousness (*viññana*) concerned with the relation of subject and object. Manas is essentially dual, its lower aspect being concerned with and directed towards the worlds of sense (*vedana, sankharas*, etc.), constituting the viññana of the perishable *skandhas* (q.v.); and the higher, attracted to and illumined by *buddhi* the faculty of intuition. This latter, differentiated by the term *bodhicitta*, is the storehouse of the experiences of the past and is the individuality, the viññana which creates the bodies and environment of the next life on earth. (v. *Viññana, Skandhas*.)

MANTRA (Sk): A formula or invocation having magical potency. Mantras are used in the Japanese Shingon and Tendai sects. Idea is based on scientific study of vibrations, but reliance on efficacy of mantras, as apart from one's innate powers, is condemned in the 3rd of the Ten Fetters.

MAYA (Sk): Literally "illusion," and popularly used in this sense, but philosophically it signifies the creative power and action which brings the phenomenal world into existence. That alone which is changeless and eternal is *real* (v. *dharmakaya*), the phenomenal universe, subject to differentiation and impermanence, is mâyâ. 2. The name of the Buddha's mother: usually called Maha-maya.

MEDITATION: Meditation plays an important part in Bsm, it being the surest way to mind-control and purification. Right Mindfulness, the sixth step on the eightfold Path, implies constant control of the thoughts, the Right Concentration, complete control of all the mental processes, resulting in *Samadhi*, the attainment of spiritual insight and tranquillity. These are the dhyanic states of superconsciousness (v. *Dhyana*). Meditation should be undertaken under the guidance of a teacher qualified by experience to give safe and suitable instruction according to the mental and physical characteristics of the pupil. Biblio: *Concentration and Meditation.* Buddhist Lodge, London, 3/6. (v. *Dhyana. Koan. Samadhi. Zen.*)

MERAYA (P): A kind of intoxicating drink referred to in the Precept against intoxication.

MERIT: The karmic result of unselfish action —mental or physical.

METTA (P): Love, active good-will for all beings, is one of the Four Divine States (*Brahmaviharas*) attained by meditation and action.

METTA SUTTA: The poem on True Friendship: *APC.* 263 and 268. (See *Some Sayings of the Buddha,* p. 65, and *S.B.E.* 10, part ii, p. 24.)

MIRACLES: In the sense of happenings resulting from the violation of natural law by an extra-cosmic being or beings, miracles are unknown in Bsm. Control of the physical world by physical methods is possible to a limited extent. Control of nature by super-physical methods through the development of the individual is possible to a much greater extent, but these methods are not supernatural and therefore not miraculous. (v. *Iddhis.*)

MOGGALLANA (P), MAUDGALYAYANA (Sk): Also called Kolita, was one of the Buddha's chief disciples—being renowned for his supernormal powers (*iddhis*); also the name of a famous B. philosopher, the author of *Prajñaptisastra.* (v. *Ananda. Sariputta.*)

MOHA (P): Mental dullness or stupidity, bewilderment, infatuation. One of the four cardinal blemishes of character. (v. *Raga. Dosa. Lobha.*)

MONDO (Jap): "Questions and answers." Term given to the short, pithy dialogues between Zen masters and their disciples. The bulk of Zen literature consists of these *mondo* and commentaries upon them.

MUDITA (P): Joy in the happiness of others. The third of the four *Brahma-viharas.*

MYSTICISM: The recognition of the essential unity of life, and conscious attainment of complete individual harmony with that unity.

Mystical philosophy is based on the concept of a transcendental monistic noumenon expressing itself through the diversity of the phenomenal. Mystical religion is the striving for complete conscious harmony with that ultimate unity: its goal is, therefore, *experience of Reality.*

This doctrine is innate in Hinayana Bsm; Anatta and Nirvana being its philosophical and religious bases. In the Mahayana School these doctrines are elaborated into a variety of forms, all endeavouring to express these fundamental truths in aspects which may appeal to every stage of mental growth and spiritual development, the one precept of all being "Look within thee, thou art Buddha!" (v. *Logos. Mahayana. Sunya. Zen.*)

NAGARJUNA (Buddhist philosopher and saint): Founder of the Madhyamika School (M.). His date is doubtful, but is placed by most authorities at beginning of 2nd c. A.D. Certain M. scriptures state him to have been a reincarnation of Ananda. Nagarjuna is often called the "Father of Mahayana," although he lived after the time of Asvaghosa, because he was first to teach the distinctively M. doctrine of *sunyata* (voidness). *Sunyata* condemns all the degrees of "realism" of the Hinayana sects, and asserts the mayavic nature of existence, in that no attributes can be predicated of the self-existent *tathata* (suchness), thus disposing of every dualism, and proclaiming the essential oneness of Nirvana and Samsara. This doctrine is presented in symbolic form in the teaching of salvation through the saving grace of Amida, which recognizes no salvation by self-effort, in that there is no "self" to strive for it. This is the "direct" method of salvation as opposed to the indirect.

Nagarjuna must not be confused with Nagasena of the *QKM*.

NANJIO: Bunyiu Nanjio, Japanese scholar. Compiler of the standard "Catalogue of the Chinese translations of the Buddhist Triptaka; the sacred Canon of the Buddhists in China and Japan," pub. Oxford 1883, photographic reprint 1929, 40/-. Works are quoted as "Nanjio No. . . ." Also author of *A Short History of the Twelve Japanese Sects*. (Tokyo, 1886.)

NEMBUTSU: Lit. "thinking of Buddha." The invocation *Namu Amida Butsu* and the act of repeating it, by which rebirth into his Paradise at death may be assured, according to the tenets of the "Pure Land" sects. Esoterically, it implies concentration on one's "Higher Self" for the purpose of attaining spiritual unity.

NEPAL: Bsm arose in the Sakya territory at the foot of the Nepal hills. Its doctrines were introduced into Nepal by Asoka, who included at least part of the country in his empire, and it was through Nepal that Bsm first entered Tibet. The Bsm of present Nepal is so corrupted by Tantric Saivism as to be a distinct religion from both. The Nepal Tarai, the "tract below the hills" along the British frontier, contains a number of interesting Buddhist ruins. (See H. A. Oldfield, *Sketches from Nipâl* (London, 1880).)

NICHIREN: Japanese religious reformer, who founded (1253) the sect called after his name. Based his teachings on the *Myoho-renge-kyo* (*Saddharma Pundarika*) alone, and taught that the very name of the scripture had mantric power, and that by meditating on the formula *Namu Myoho-renge-kyo!* and repeating it as an invocation with the realization that you yourself are potentially Buddha, the barriers of the false self are removed and enlightenment is attained. He still has a large following in Japan. the sect having over 5,000 temples. v. *B.E.*, v. p. 51 and *Nichiren, the Buddhist Prophet.* (Anesaki.)

NIDANAS (P): The Twelve Nidanas are links in the chain of karmic causation, the Buddhist method of demonstrating the reign of law in the psychophysical realms of existence. The word *Nidana* means "a link or fetter," and is appropriately used, therefore, to describe the processes by which a being comes into existence, and which bind him to the Wheel of Life. Being a "Wheel," there is no actual starting-point, but as Ignorance is the primary root of existence, and because its complete removal is essential for escape from rebirth, it is usually placed first. The formula then runs:—

On *Avijjâ*—Ignorance—depends *Sankhârâ.*

On *Sankhârâ*—the karmic results of such illusion—depends *Viññâna.*

On *Viññâna*—individual consciousness—depends *Nâma-Rûpa.*

On *Nâma-Rûpa*—Mind, and its expression in Form—depends *Salâyatana.*

On *Salâyatana*—the six sense organs and their appropriate functions—depends *Phassa.*

On *Phassa*—touch; the sense, the object, and the sense impression—depends *Vedanâ.*

On *Vedanâ*—feeling, sensation—depends *Tanhâ.*

On *Tanhâ*—thirst, craving for personal experience—depends *Upâdâna.*

On *Upâdâna*—grasping, clinging to existence—depends *Bhava.*

On *Bhava*—becoming and rebecoming—depends *Jâti.*

On *Jâti*—birth: the final outcome of *kamma*—depends

Jarâmarana (with *soka-parideva-dukkha-domanass' upayâsâ*) Old age and Death, with tribulation, grief, sorrow, distress, despair.

This chain has to be broken by the elimination of *Tanha* (thirst for personal existence), this being the first step towards the complete elimination of ignorance and the attainment of Enlightenment, which brings freedom from rebirth into psycho-physical existence.

The technical term for the Nidana Chain is *Paticca-samuppâda* (arising on the grounds of a preceding cause; dependent origination).

The oldest form of the Chain contains ten links only, *Avijja* and *Sankhara* being absent. See *Mahâpadâna Sutto* (*Dial.* II, 24 sqq.) Biblio: *Word of the Buddha*, Nyanatiloka. *W.B.*, pp. 76-81. Nidanas and Astrology. v. *B.E.*, 12, 2, p. 41. (v. *Wheel of Life.*)

NIHILISM: The philosophic doctrine that denies a substantial reality to the phenomenal universe. Bsm takes the middle path between the realists (*âstika*), who maintain the universe to be real, and the non-realists (*nâstika*), who deny all reality. The Buddha condemned both the *âstika* and the *nâstika* concepts. v. *Dial I.*, pp. 26 sqq. See also Holmes, *Creed of Buddha*, pp. 217-231.)

NIRMANAKAYA (Sk): v. The "body of transformation," by which the Bodhisattva remains in contact with phenomenal existence for the helping of humanity on its pilgrimage. The condition of the Dharmakaya (q.v.) in manifestation (*Samsara*), as distinct from its condition in Nirvana (*Sambhogakaya*, q.v.). (v. *Trikaya.*)

NIRVANA (Sk), NIBBANA (P): The supreme Goal of Buddhist endeavour; release from the limitations of existence. The word is derived from a root which signifies "Extinguished through lack of fuel," and since rebirth is the result of egoistic desire (*tanha*), freedom from rebirth is attained by the extinguishing of all such desire. Nirvana is, therefore, a state attainable in this life by right aspiration, purity of life, and the elimination of egoism. One who has attained to this state is called a saint or arhat (q.v.) and at the death of his physical body attains complete or final nirvana (*parinibbana* or *anupadisesa nirvana*) in which all attributes relating to phenomenal existence cease, and which is, therefore, called *sunyata* or void. This is cessation of existence, as we know existence; the attainment of Being (as distinct from becoming); union with Ultimate Reality. This is the goal of all mystic endeavour, and mystics of every creed speak of it as "a state which passeth all understanding." The Christian mystic Molinos spoke of it as "the annihilation of the soul in the ecstasy of divine union." In the Buddhist scriptures (*Udana* ch. 8, p. 112 of Strong's trsl.) the Buddha speaks of it as "an unborn, unoriginated, uncreated, unformed," contrasting it with the born, originated, created and formed phenomenal world.

The Hinayana School tends to view Nirvana as escape from life by overcoming its attractions: the Mahayana views it as the fruition of life—the unfolding of the infinite possibilities of the innate Buddha-nature—, and exalts the saint who remains in touch with life, rather than the saint who relinquishes all connection with it.

Biblio: Any work on Bsm deals with the subject, but the following are helpful: Refs. in *W.B.*, especially pp. 148-155. Outlines of Mahayana *Bsm* (see Index), Stcherbatsky: *Conceptions of Buddhist Nirvana.* Hare: *Mysticism of East and West* (ch. xi).

NUMERICAL STRENGTH OF BSM: Impossible to ascertain the number of adherents of Bsm. Rh. D. in *Buddhism* (S.P.C.K.), pp. 4-6, gives Hinayana 30 millions, and Mahayana 470 millions. Later statistics vary between 180 millions and 455 millions. The higher estimates include the bulk of the Chinese as Buddhist, but the masses follow a degarded Taoism, and the majority of the cultured class follow Confucianism. (v. *China.*) If we include only half the population of China, we arrive at a total of about 300 millions, or one-fifth the population of the world, which may be taken as a reasonably accurate estimation.

OLCOTT, H. S.: Founder with H. P. Blavatsky of Theosophical Society. Organizer of the last Buddhist revival in Ceylon. (v. *Ceylon.*) Author of *Buddhist Catechism,* and compiler of the Fourteen Fundamental Buddhist Beliefs (q.v.).

PADMA SAMBHAVA: The "Lotus Born," a native of N. India, established Lamaism in Tibet. He belonged to the ritualistic and mystical Yogacharaya sect founded by Aryasangha, and he went to Tibet in 747 A.D. from Nalanda University at the invitation of Khri-Srong, the then king of Tibet. His influence is considered by some students, and by many followers of the Gelugpa sect, to have been a detrimental one, but Waddell (in *E.R.E.* vii, 785) says that the remarkably high literary standard of the translations of the Canon, a work organized and supervised by him, goes to disprove this idea. The idea probably arose from the fact that all sects, even the lowest dugpas, claim Padma Sambhava as their founder.

PALI: One of the "sacred" languages of Bsm. The language in which the *Pitakas* (q.v.) were first committed to writing. See *Sakya,* Mrs. Rh. D., p. 429. James Gray, *Pali Grammar,* Parts 1 & 2. Calcutta. (v. *Kosala.*)

PALI CANON: v. *Tipitaka.* For history and critical study of the Pali Canon, see Winternitz, *History of Indian Literature, vol. II,* 1927.

PALI TEXT SOCIETY: Founded by Professor T. W. Rhys Davids, 1881, to publish Buddhist Pali texts and commentaries in a Roman script transliteration, and to publish translations of same into English. It is expected that the entire Pali Canon and the major commentaries will be translated into English by 1941. Also a Pali-English Dictionary in four volumes. A " Journal " is published yearly. Subscription from one guinea per annum. Hon. Secretary, Mrs. C. A. F. Rhys Davids, Chipstead, Surrey (Eng.).

PANNA (P), PRAJNA (Sk): Wisdom, insight.

PANSIL: *Pañcha Sila,* Five Precepts. The five Moral Rules which every Buddhist, layman and bhikkhu, promises to observe. They enjoin compassion, honesty, purity, sincerity, and temperance. It is customary in most Buddhist lands to recite the Precepts in the original Pali, thus:—

1.—*Pânâtipâtâ veramani sikkhâpadaṁ samâdiyâmi.*

2.—*Adinnâdânâ veramani sikkhâpadaṁ samâdiyâmi.*

3.—*Kâmesu micchâcârâ veramani sikkhâpadam saṁâdiyâmi.*

4.—*Musâwâdâ veramani sikkhâpadam samâdiyâmi.*

5.—*Surâ-merayâ-majja-paṁâda-tthânâ veramani sikkhâpadaṁ saṁâdiyâmi.*

Translation: I undertake to keep the rule (of training) which enjoins abstinence from (1) Injuring or killing any living thing; (2) taking that which is not given; (3) immoral sensual enjoyment; (4) false speech; (5) intoxication as tending to cloud the mind.

Note that vowels have Italian values; c=ch; v=a sound between English v and w; final m is a nasal sound very similar to " ng " in " hung." (v. *B.E.* vol. I, 145, and vol. II, 135.)

PARAMITAS (Sk): Perfections. The six (or ten) stages of spiritual perfection followed by the Bodhisattva in his progress to Buddahood. They include the practice and highest possible development of charity, morality, patient resignation, zeal, meditation and contemplation, wisdom. The following four are sometimes added: skilful means of teaching, power over obstacles, spiritual aspiration, and knowledge, these last four being, however, regarded as amplifications of *Prajña*, wisdom.

PATIMOKKHA (P): The 227 disciplinary rules binding on the bhikkhu, and recited on *Uposatha* days for purposes of confession. These are enumerated in the *Suttavibhanga*, the first part of the *Vinaya Pitaka*. See *S.B.E.* xiii, pp. 1-69.

PESSIMISM: The philosophic doctrine that the Universe is fundamentally evil. Bsm asserts that sorrow or evil is due to ignorance of the true nature of Being and false conceptions of "self," and teaches the way out of sorrow into the happiness and peace of Nirvana. (v. Holmes, *Creed of Buddha*, pp. 207-211 & *W.B.*, p. 35.)

PETAVATTHU: The seventh work in the *Khuddaka Nikaya* (APC. 274). It deals with rebirth in the peta worlds as the *Vimana-vatthu* (APC. 273) deals with rebirth in the Celestial worlds. *The Buddhist Conception of Spirits*, B. C. Law (1923), comprises summaries of both of these works.

PHILOSOPHIC BASIS OF BUDDHISM: Buddhism is a way of life; a discipline: not a system of dogmas to be accepted by the intellect. It is a way to *live Reality*, and not ideas concerning the nature of Reality.

Bsm is concerned with this life. It therefore encourages man to understand the world in which he lives, but it emphatically bids man not to consider this life an end in itself; not to be bound to it. Clinging to life as though it were Reality: desiring the experiences of life as though they were real and good: these are illusions.

Bsm therefore emphasizes the transitoriness and ill of life, and teaches the Way to the conscious experience of the Reality of which it is only a finite expression.

From this follows the idea that if an individual is to transcend this phenomenal realm and experience the Real (*Nirvana*), he must be in his essential nature one with that transcendental Reality; for the Real cannot be created out of the unreal, nor can the finite comprehend the Infinite.

Buddhist philosophy has been concerned principally with the nature of the Real and the relationship between the real and the unreal, the phenomenal and the noumenal, and speculation on this problem has ranged from the most extreme form of Realism which asserted this phenomenal world to be Reality, to the most extreme form of idealism, which denied all reality to the phenomenal world. The Middle Path between the two, the monism of the Mahayana Schools, sees existence as one aspect of Reality, the phenomenal and the noumenal being but two sides or poles of one transcendental eternal reality which unifies both. See *Buddhist Philosophy*, A. B. Keith: *Outlines of Mahayana Bsm*, Suzuki.

PILGRIMS: A pilgrimage with a religious motive is considered an act of merit. Famous Buddhist pilgrims were Fa Hian (399-413), Hiuen Tsiang (629-645), I-Tsing (671-695), Chinese bhikkhus from China to India, and Sung Yün, a layman, sent from China to study Indian Bsm (c. 518 A.D.). See works of S. Beal for accounts of these pilgrims.

Buddhist Pilgrim's Progress: a famous Chinese work of religious fiction based on the pilgrimage of Hiuen Tsiang. Abridged translations by T. Richard, *A Mission to Heaven*, and Helen M. Hayes, *The Buddhist Pilgrim's Progress*. The *Pilgrimage of Bsm*, important work by Dr. J. B. Pratt (1928).

PIPRAWA: In 1898, a stupa was unearthed at Piprawa, just over the Nepalese frontier, which contained, among other objects, a steatite vase containing pieces of charred bone, with an inscription which was translated as asserting that the remains were relics of the Buddha. The stupa was assumed to be that erected by the Sakyas of Kapilavatthu over their share of the ashes of the Buddha, but some doubt was later thrown on the assumption owing to differences of opinion regarding the exact meaning of the inscription. The subject is discussed in the pages of *Buddhism in England* for the year 1931. The stupa was discovered by Mr. W. C. Peppé on his estate, and is often referred to as the " Peppé stupa."

PITAKAS: Pitaka=basket. The Buddhist Pali Canon is called the Pitakas, or the Tipitaka (three baskets). These are called Sutta P., Abhidhamma P., and Vinaya P. Applied in the sense of " handing on," as baskets are used to hand on earth in excavation work. For details of Pitakas see the Lodge publication *An Analysis of the Pali Canon.*

PITI (P): Interest and joy in the service of others. Cp. *muditâ.*

PRAJNA (Sk), PANNA (P): Transcendental wisdom, divine intuition. One of the Six Paramitas (q.v.). (v. *Wisdom.*)

PRAJNAPARAMITAS (Sk): A group of M. scriptures: the sutras on the " perfection of wisdom by divine intuition." They comprise a number of works, the best-known being: the *Mahaprajñaparamita Sutra,* the *Ashtasaharika-prajñaparamita,* the larger and smaller *Prajñaparamitahridaya Sutras,* and the *Vajracchedika.* See *S.B.E.* 49, and Buddhist Lodge pamphlet "*Mahayana Buddhist Scriptures*" (in preparation). Also see Appendix to *Aspects of Mahayana Buddhism,* Nalinaksha Dutt, pp. 323-335.

PRAYER, in the sense of intercession, petition to an external deity for personal benefits, is unknown in Bsm. Meditation (q.v.) takes its place.

PRECEPTS: There are ten moral " precepts " or pledges. These are correctly called *dasasikkhâpadâni,* and pledge those who take them, not to: (1) take life, (2) steal, (3) indulge in sensuality, (4) lie, (5) become intoxicated by drink or drugs, (6) eat at unseasonable times, (7) attend worldly amusements, (8) use perfumes or wear ornaments, (9) sleep on a luxurious bed, (10) possess gold or silver.

The first Five Precepts (v. *Pansil*) were originally binding on all who entered the Sangha: later, other five were added, the ten being binding on all bhikkhus, novices being bound by the first five only. Later, it became the custom for the pious layman to take the first five, and these are now considered as the minimum moral code to be followed by all who call themselves Buddhists. Public recital of the "Three Refuges" and the "Five Precepts" is the outward form of "becoming a Buddhist." On Uposatha Days and at Wesak, the lay disciple often keeps the first eight of the Ten Precepts. This is called *atthangika uposatha.*

Note that the "Precepts" are not commandments, the basic idea being that of an influence from within, not a command from without. They are aspirations or vows (to one's higher self).

PURE LAND SCHOOL: Founded as White Lotus Sect in China by Hui-yüan (c. 400 A.D.): introduced Japan by Honen (1133-1211). Pure Land (*Ching T'u*: Jap. *Jôdô-shu*) doctrine personifies the Higher Self or Buddha-nature as Bodhisattva Amitabha (Amida), teaching that Faith in Amida and prayer to him will ensure rebirth in his Western Paradise (Sukhavati), the "Pure Land," where the attainment of Nirvana is easy and certain. The Shin-shiu (sect), founded by Honen's disciple Shinran, teaches salvation by mere repetition of name of Amida (Nembutsu), the mantrum being "*Namu Amida Butsu.*" Scriptures are: Asvaghosa's *A.F.M.*, the short and long *Sukhavati Sutras*, and *Amitayurdhyana Sutra*, with the *Kyô-gyô-shin-sho* by Shinran for the Shin Sect. See *A Study of Shin Bsm.*, by Sasaki (Kyoto). (v. *Christianity, Japan.*)

QUESTIONS OF KING MILINDA: (*Milinda Pañha*) Records of discussions on the principles of Bsm between the Greek king Menander (Milinda) and the Buddhist *thera* Nâgasena. Probably written in Pali c. 100 B.C. Although non-canonical, QKM. was acknowledged as authoritative by Buddhaghosa; this being the only work outside the Pali Canon he thus recognized. Trsl. Rh. D. *Questions of King Milinda, S.B.E.* xxxv. xxxvi. For a critical study of the work, see *The Milinda-Questions.* Mrs. Rh. D. (1930).

RAGA (P): Passion; uncontrolled lust of every kind: with *dosa* and *moha* forming the three cardinal blemishes of character; *lobha,* greed, being often added as a fourth.

RAHULA: The name of the Buddha's son, born shortly before he left his home on his quest for enlightenment. Rahula entered the Sangha at about the age of 15 and became one of the 12 "Elders." *Thera-Gatha* 296 records his attainment of Arahatship. Suttas entitled Rahula are *APC.* 95, 96, 181, 204, the first of these being the famous one against falsehood (see *Further Dialogues* I, p. 297).

REALITY: (v. *Tathata. Nirvana.*)

REBIRTH: An ancient Indian doctrine which the Buddha embodied in his own teaching in a modified form. The term Rebirth is used in Bsm to distinguish it from transmigration, for the latter implies the return to earth in a new body of a distinct entity which may be called a soul. In Bsm Rebirth is the corollary of Karma (q.v.); i.e., no spiritual or psychic entity passes from life to life, but each life must be considered the karmic effect of the previous life and the cause of the following life. The karma which causes man to return again and again to this world in a cycle of rebirths is the result of *tanha* (q.v.). Desiring life and shunning death, man creates an opposition between them; consequently he is "thrown" from one to the other until he can bring this opposition to an end. Rebirth is also explained by reference to the law of cycles. Just as night and day, waking and sleeping, alternate in an endless series, so also do the life and death of that karmic wave which is called the individual. The wave has its ups and downs and appears to be moving forward. Actually the substance of the wave does not go forward; only the movement goes forward, and by this analogy is explained the Buddhist paradox that there can be Rebirth without any entity or soul that is reborn. Biblio: *W.B.* p. 92 *et seq.* (v. *Karma, Anatta, Nirvana, Wheel of Life.*)

RELICS: The veneration of relics began immediately after the *parinibbana* of the Buddha, religious pilgrimages being made to the ten stupas erected over his ashes, and to the Four Holy Places. Stupas were also erected over the ashes of *arhats*, and these became objects of veneration.

The famous "Tooth Relic" is preserved at the Dalada Maligawa Temple, near Kandy. Its vicissitudes have been so bound up with Sinhalese history for over 2,000 years, that the relic has acquired a national significance which outweighs any personal import it may originally have had. Biblio. *Dathavamsa* (*History of the Tooth Relic*). B. C. Law and W. Stede. (v. *Piprawa.*)

RELIGION: Bsm is classed as one of the five great religions of the world, but is sometimes said to be a system of moral philosophy rather than a religion. If a personal deity, the creator and ruler of the universe, is essential to a concept of religion, with a mythology and system of magic connected with his relationship thereto, then Bsm is not a religion. If, however, we conceive of Reality as Universal Law, and religion as a system by which the individual is brought into harmony with that Universal Law, then Bsm may be classed as such. See *W.B.*, pp. 12, 13, 83, 160, 169.

RENUNCIATION: Sacrifice of self-interest, the only kind of sacrifice recognized as of any value in treading the Path. The two great Renunciations in the life of the Buddha are: (1) The renunciation of home, family and kingdom, and (2) the renunciation of Nirvana at the "Enlightenment," and the determination to teach the Good Law. The esoteric schools of the Mahayana add a third: the renunciation of *parinibbana* and the taking of the Nirmanakaya vesture. (v. *Bodhisattva. Trikaya.*)

REVELATION: Bsm recognizes no revelation in the sense of a disclosure of Truth to mankind by favour of a deity. Revelation of Truth is attained by each individual for and by himself by removal of error from the mind and its consequent illumination or "Enlightenment."

RITUAL: Early Bsm deprecated ritual, and the Southern School still makes little use of ceremony of any kind. Certain sects of the Mahayana, notably the Lamaism of Tibet and the Tendai and Shingon sects of Japan, use elaborate rituals. In so far as these are believed to render self-discipline unnecessary they are hindrances on the Path, but if used as aids to concentration and the upliftment of the mind they may be helpful to certain temperaments. (v. *Fetters. Magic.*)

RUMMINDEI: The site of the Lumbini Garden where the Buddha was born: Across the Nepalese border, E. 85° 11, N. 25° 58. The pillar erected by Asoka with the inscription, signifying, "Here the Blessed One was born," is still standing.

RUPA (P & Sk): Form. *Arupa,* formless. Form implies limitation, and form as cognized by the lower mind persists into the lower heaven worlds. The higher heaven worlds are called formless because the mind is free from the limitations of the senses. Desire for life in the worlds of form (*ruparaga*) is the sixth Fetter to be cast off, and *aruparaga* the seventh. (v. *Four Paths. Rupa,* an image.)

RYOBU SHINTO (Jap): Two-sided Shinto (as contrasted with Yuiitsu Shinto). The fusion of Bsm with Shinto effected by Dengyo Daishi and Kobo Daishi in the 9th c. A.D. in Japan. By this Shinto and Bsm were shown to be but two sides of the same basic truths, the ancestral Sun Goddess Amaterasu, was made identical with the Dhyani Buddha Vairochana (*Dainichi*), and the lesser Shinto deities were declared to be manifestations of attributes of the Eternal Adi-Buddha. This union lasted until the "Restoration" in 1868, when Shinto was restored as the State religion and efforts were made to suppress Bsm. In 1872, however, complete religious liberty was established, and Buddhist and Shinto priests were equally recognised as "Kyodoshoku" (official moral instructors). See *Ryobu Shinto*, Mori, *B.E.*, October, 1931.

SACRED: In Bsm there is no division of life into the dualism of sacred and profane, or of good and evil. (v. *Evil.*) Veneration is shown for holiness of life, especially for the basic virtue of altruism.

SACRED BOOKS OF THE BUDDHISTS: A series of publications comprising the Jatakamala, and the Dialogues of the Buddha. Founded by Max Muller, and continued after his death by Mrs. Rh. D. Published by Oxford University Press.

SACRED BOOKS OF THE EAST: Series (ed. Max Muller) also by O.U.P. Buddhist volumes are Nos. 10, 11, 13, 17, 19, 20, 21, 35, 36 & 49.

SADDHARMA PUNDARIKA: One of the Nine Dharmas (q.v.) of the Mahayana School. Eng. trsls.: *The Lotus of the True Law*, by Kern. from the Sk. (*S.B.E.*, vol. 21), *and The Lotus of the Wonderful Law*, abridged version by Soothill from the Chinese (*Miao-Fa Lien Hua Ching*). (Oxford, 1930). Teaches the identification of the historical Buddha with the transcendental Buddha existing from the beginning of this cosmic age, his appearance in he phenomenal worlds being only a skilful device (*upâya*) adopted to preach the dharma to mankind.

Salvation is attained by the grace of the Bodhisattvas, the Hinayana method of salvation being inadequate.

A synopsis of the S.P. is given in *B.E.*, vol. VI. (see Index). Also see Richard, *New Testament of Higher Bsm* (1910).

Date: the "Lotus" was first translated into Chinese in 255 A.D. Authorities place the original at about 150-170 A.D.

SAKYA: The clan to which the Buddha belonged. From *shâka,* the sal-tree (*Shorea robusta*). The Shakyans were the people of the sal-forest tracts. Some doubt has been expressed as to their being of pure Aryan descent. They were not ruled by kings as were the majority of the Aryan states, but were republicans led by chieftains called rajas, the father of the Buddha being such a ruler. They made their own laws, meeting at the Moot Hall for this purpose. They were monogamous, and did not recognize the caste rules of the Hindus.

SAKYAMUNI, the Sage of the Sakyas: a title often applied to the Buddha by those outside the Sakyan clan.

SAKKAYADITTHI (P): The belief that in one or all of the five *Skandhas* (q.v.) there is an individuality or self, an *atta.* The first of the Ten Fetters (v. *Four Paths*). cp. *Attavada.*

SAMADHI (P & Sk): Contemplation on Reality. The state of spiritual ecstasy consequent on complete elimination of all sense of separateness, resulting from continued meditation on Reality. It is superior to meditation in that the three factors of meditation (the mind of the individual, the object of meditation, and the relationship between them) are transcended. *Samma samadhi,* perfect contemplation, is the last stage of the Noble Eightfold Path, and the prelude to Nirvana. (v. *Nirvana.*)

SAMBHOGAKAYA (Sk): The noumenal or "Bliss Body" of the triune Dharmakaya: the vehicle of the creative force of the universe poured forth for humanity through the Buddha as Nirmanakaya. Also the condition of the Dharmakaya in Nirvana as distinct from Nirmanakaya, its condition in manifestation (*samsara*). (v. *Trikaya.*)

SAMBODHI (P): The insight, wisdom, and assimilation of Truth essential to the attainment of the three higher stages of arhatship. The seven qualities or attributes of *sambodhi* are: self-control, understanding of the *dhamma*, zeal, tranquillity of mind, joy, concentration, compassion. *Samma sambodhi* is the supreme spiritual insight of a Buddha. See *Dial. I,* 190-2.

SAMKHARAS (P) (also spelt *Samskaras*): The second link in the Nidana Chain, and the fourth of the Five Skandhas. Mental predispositions; the karmic results of mental illusion. The congeries of mental properties which collectively make up awareness, or the elements of consciousness. See *Compendium of Philosophy,* pp. 273-276. (v. *Nidana. Skandhas.*)

SAMMA (P): Supreme; the highest point or summit. The highest form of attainment possible. In its *relative* meaning it is used to describe each step of the Noble Eightfold Path, being usually translated "Right." Here it means the highest state possible for any given individual to attain, according to his mental and moral development and his environment. In its *absolute* sense it means "supreme," as in the invocation: *Namo tassa Bhagavato Arahato Sammâ Sambuddhassa!* Homage to him, Blessed One, Worthy One, Supreme in Highest Wisdom (Supremely Enlightened).

SAMMITIYAS: A Buddhist sect and school, holding a specific doctrine and a special discipline.

They are referred to in the Kathavatthu, in several Tibetan sources, and by Hiouen Tsiang, who estimated their numbers in the 7th c. as about 43,000 bhikkhus. They were a Hinayana sect and are interesting chiefly on account of their views on *anatta*.

The Sammitiyas believed in a form of reincarnation by which some entity superior to the Five Skandhas passed over from life to life. This entity was not a permanent soul-entity, but it was superior to the *skandhas* in that it transmigrated as the vehicle of character. They supported their views on the attitude of the Buddha to the soul theory, in that he never denied or affirmed a soul, and also on the "sutta of the burden bearer," *Sam. N.* xxii, 22 (see Warren B.T. § 23a). The only literature of the sect now extant is the *Sammitiyasastra,* which exists at present only in Chinese. *v. Viññana.*

SAMSARA (P & Sk) (also spelt *Sangsara*): Lit. "faring on," continued "coming-to-be." Samsara, as *Existence,* is contrasted with Nirvana, *Being,* the one being subject to all the limitations of "becoming," the other being the state of pure "Being" (or Be-ness). Nirvana is symbolically referred to as "the further shore of the ocean of samsara"; the *dhamma* as the raft which carries us across. *Samsaracakka*: the wheel of rebirth.

SAMYUTTA NIKAYA: The third of the five main divisions of the *Sutta Pitaka.* It consists of 56 *Samyuttas* divided into five "Vaggas" or series. See APC. p. 7. The first four "Vaggas" have appeared in English under the title of the *Book of the Kindred Sayings.* The fifth is in preparation.

SANGHA: An Assembly. The monastic order founded by the Buddha, the members of which are called bhikkhus (m) or bhikkhunis (f). It is the oldest monastic order in the world. The act of admission to the Order is called *pabajjâ* (renouncing the world). The hair of the head and the beard are shaved, the yellow robe (consisting of three garments) is donned, and the *Tisarana* is recited. The person is then a novice. The ordination ceremony (*upasampadâ*) takes place before a chapter of at least ten senior bhikkhus (*theras*). No oaths are taken, and the bhikkhu is free to leave the Order at any time if he desires to do so. The bhikkhu possesses only his robes, alms-bowl, razor, needle and water-strainer. He eats only one meal a day, no food being taken after mid-day. Biblio: *Early Buddhist Monachism*, S. Dutt, *W.B.*, pp. 211-216. (v. *Bhikkhu. Patimokkha.*)

In the Mahayana School, the Sangha tends to become recognized as a spiritual unity rather than a physical one. The ideal Sangha is the community of followers of the Dhamma in the world, rather than an exclusive few who retire from the world. The monastic system is strong in Tibet, but is dying out in China and Japan. Monasteries exist in most M. sects, but they are training colleges for *bhikkhus* rather than retreats from the world. Bhikkhus of M. sects keep few Vinaya Rules, and often marry. They are teachers rather than monks.

SANTIDEVA: One of the most important of the later writers of the Mahayana School. He lived in the 7th c. A.D., and compiled two important works of M. doctrine, entitled *Siksha-Samuccaya* and *Bodhicharyavatara*. The former is a compendium of the true doctrine of the M. School. It is compiled from over a hundred earlier M. works, many of them no longer extant. The latter work deals with the rules of discipline for those following the Bodhisattva Path of the M. School. Bendall: *Siksha-Samuccaya* (Ldn.), 1922. Barnett: *Path of Light* (Ldn.), 1909.

Both works teach the superiority of the way of the Bodhisattva, and the doctrine of the void (*sunya*).

SARIPUTTA (P), SARIPUTRA (Sk): Also called Upatissa. One of the two chief disciples of the Buddha. Known as *Dhammasenāpati*, the "Captain of the Dhamma," he was acknowledged by the Buddha as next to Himself in the "Turning of the Wheel of the Law." Several discourses in the scriptures are attributed to Sariputta, e.g., *Dig. N.* iii, 210 and 272, *Maj. N.* i, 13 and *Ang. N.* ii, 160, also several M. scriptures. Also see *Sam. N.* xii, 85.

Sariputta was converted by Assaji (see *Vinaya Texts* I, 144-151).

The ashes of S. were found, with those of Moggalana, in one of the stupas at Sanchi (q.v.).

SAKADAGAMIN (P): v. *Four Paths.*

SARNATH: One of the Four Holy Places of Bsm. The present name of the extensive Buddhist ruins, near Dhamekh (N. 25° 23′ E. 83° 2′) 3½ miles N. of Benares, believed to be the site of the Deer Park Isipattana, where the Buddha preached his first Sermon to the five ascetics. One of the Asokan pillars was found here. The Anagarika Dharmapala constructed a vihara here, called the Mulagandhakuti Vihara, which was opened in 1931.

SATORI (Jap): A Zen term for the sudden flash of Enlightenment which, as a rule, follows successful concentration on a Ko-an, q.v. There are instances in Zen literature of *satori* coming without the Ko-an, but these are rare. In every case, however, *s.* is realized with the final "letting-go" which comes at the end of prolonged and intense search for Enlightenment.

SCRIPTURES: v. *Canon. QKM. Japan. Pali Canon.*

SECTS: There are two great Schools, the Hinayana and the Mahayana. The former is divided into a few sects which differ mainly on points of monastic discipline. (v. *Burma. Ceylon. Siam.*) The Mahayana is divided into the Lamaism of

Tibet and Mongolia, and the Buddhism of China and Japan, the latter being divided into salvation through one's own efforts (Jap. *jiriki*), and through the efforts of another (*Jap. tariki*). These two divisions are subdivided into a number of sects. (v. *Japan.*) The only sect showing a sectarian spirit is the *Nichiren* (q.v.). All others emphasize various aspects of dhamma, but view all other doctrines as equally true. (v. *Tendai.*)

SHINGON-SHU: The sect of the True Word. Japanese Buddhist sect founded on the doctrines of the Chinese *Chen-yen* (founded 716 A.D.), but differing in many important respects from it and its Indian predecessor. It was established in Japan by Kukai (posthumously named Kobodaishi), c. 806 A.D. Kukai was a great harmonizer, seeing every religion as an expression of definite stages in the great pilgrimage of humanity to the self-realization of Buddahood. He divided these stages into ten, from the lowest state of the man absorbed in material things, in whom the Buddha-nature had hardly begun to function, to the highest state of Shingon mysticism, the state of the soul which has awakened to the glories of cosmic mysteries and lives the Buddha-life here on earth. The "Hinayana" stage comes fourth in his scheme. The Shingon doctrine is a pantheistic mysticism which sees the universe as an expression of ultimate reality, its goal the fruition of the Buddha-nature in the heart of man. It relies largely on magical ritual, such as the use of invocations (*mantras*) and hand poses (*mudras*). The mantras are in a debased Sanskrit, many being kept secret, and known only to the initiated priests of the sect. In doctrine and in practice (Ref. *Annales du Musée Guimet*, Vol. viii) Shingon has much in common with Brahminism, Gnosticism and Kabbalism. The Supreme Reality is personified in Vairocana Buddha, the Buddha Sakamuni being viewed as a partial manifestation of Vairochana. The chief scriptures of

Shingon are *Mahavairscana Sutra* and *Vajrashekhara Sutra.*

Kikai was a great religious genius and social reformer, a clever engineer and artist. He was instrumental, with Dengyo Daishi, in establishing the union of Shinto with Buddhism known as Ryobu Shinto (q.v.). He died at the great monastery founded by him on Mount Koya, still the headquarters of Shingon. See *B.E.*, Vol. V, pp. 172 and 175.

The sect is an important one, having about 13,000 temples in Japan. Biblio: (v. *Japan.*)

SHINRAN SHONIN: Jap. 1173-1262. Founder of the Jodo-Shin sect. A disciple of Honen (Jodo sect) he carried the doctrine of salvation by faith in Amida to the extreme of mere repetition of the name of Amida. He advocated marriage of priests, and himself lived the married life. He popularized congregational worship, and wrote about 400 hymns (*wa-san* or *gathas*) for use at the temple services. He also wrote the *Kyôgyôshinshô Monrui*, in six volumes, which deals exhaustively with the cardinal doctrines of Jodo-shin Buddhism. Died Kyoto 1262; posthumous name, conferred by Emperor in 1876, Kenshin Daishi. (v. *Jodo. Hongwanji.*) See Sasaki, *Shin Buddhism*, pp. 97-139.

SHIN SHU: The name of the Japanese "Pure Land" or Amida sects. (v. *Jodo, Pure Land, Shinran Shonin, Honen.*) See G. Sasaki, A *Study of Shin Buddhism* (Tokyo, 1925).

SHOTOKU (TAISHI): Prince Regent to the Empress Suiko (572-621), the Prince Shôtoku is reverenced by Japanese Buddhists as the first imperial patron of their religion. A great statesman, theologian and missionary, he has been called the "Asoka of Japan." (v. *Japan.*)

SIAM: Bsm was introduced into Siam via Cambodia about the year 422 A.D. The Siamese are very earnest in their religious beliefs, and there have been no periods of decline or deterioration. The doctrine is that of the S. or Hinayana School. The standard work on doctrine, after the Pali Canon, is the *Trai Phûm*, a compilation in Siamese of works and commentaries on the Pali Canon. The ruler exercises authority over the monasteries and himself nominates the *Sangkharat* or head of the Sangha. King Mongkut reformed the Sangha, and encouraged the study of Pali, and his son, King Chulalongkorn, had the whole of the Tipitaka printed in 39 volumes at Bangkok in 1893, and distributed copies lavishly amongst the scholars and libraries of Europe and America. The Buddhist monastery is called a "wat," and the Siamese word for bhikkhu is *phiku* or *phisu*, but they are usually given the title "phra," great one. See Alabaster, *Wheel of the Law*, Young, *Kingdom of the Yellow Robe*, pp. 251-387.

Siam is the only Buddhist kingdom existing to-day. The population is about nine millions, of whom about one million are Malays professing the Muhammedan religion.

SILA (P & Sk): (1) Habit, behaviour, nature, character, e.g., *adânasila*, not-giving-nature = stingy; *pâpasila*, evil-nature = wicked. (2) Moral precepts, code of morality, Buddhist ethics. *Pañcha-sila*, the Five Precepts; *dasa-sila*, the Ten Precepts. (v. *Precepts*.)

One of the moral "Trinity." *Sila*, right deeds, *Dana*, benevolence, *Bhavana*, purification and discipline of the mind, from which *Pañña*, wisdom, follows. (v. *Pansil*.)

Dasa Sila, the ten points of good character, are: (1) To avoid taking life; (2) to avoid stealing; (3) to avoid indulgence in sensuality; (4) to avoid lying; (5) to avoid intoxication; (6) to avoid slandering and reviling others; (7) to avoid self-praise and frivolous talk; (8) to avoid avarice and covetousness; (9) to avoid enmity and malevolence; (10)

to avoid heretical views, and deriding the Buddha, the Dhamma, the Sangha.

SKANDHAS (Sk), KHANDHA (P): Original meaning, bulk or mass. Derived meaning, a congeries or collection of parts forming in combination a specific object; e.g., body, wheels, axles, etc., form a vehicle if combined; separately they are only a collection of units. Technical meaning: the five causally conditioned elements of existence forming a being or entity. In the personal sense, the skandhas are the elements which condition the appearance of life in any form; which together make up the personality in the sphere of *samsara*. The Five Skandhas are inherent in every form of life, either in an active or a potential state; e.g., there is consciousness in the mineral, but it is dormant. In man, all five elements are active. These are enumerated as: (1) *Rupa*, (2) *Vedanâ*, (3) *Sañña*, (4) *Sankhâra*, (5) *Viññâna*.

These are all material, in the sense of being subject to the characteristics of existence, *anicca, dukkha, anatta*. They form the temporal or phenomenal nature of man, and it is the idea or belief that separately or collectively they form a self or ego that is the heresy of *sakayaditthi*, the first of the "Ten Fetters" which bind men to the Wheel of Life. See Warren, *Bsm in Trsl.*, pp. 129-147, and Holmes, *Creed of Buddha*, 187-200.

Rupa: Form, body, shape. A limited space, a limitation in any sphere of (personal) existence. Rupa is not physical alone, there is a psychical rupa, a mental rupa, etc., but in considering the five skandhas, it is usual to consider Rupa as the material body composed of physical and etheric matter.

Vedanâ: Feeling or sensation; the emotional body.

Saññâ: Perception; awareness of, and assimilation of sensation.

Sankhârâ (samkharas): The mental impressions resulting from vedanâ and saññâ. The elements of consciousness.

Viññâna: Consciousness, the relation between subject and object. Mind as creator of personality.

The three last elements constitute the lower or concrete mind. For the higher mind, see *viññâna* and *bodhi*.

The skandhas dissolve after death so that the memory of personal experiences is not brought over to the next physical life. The result of that experience is, however, built into, or assimilated by the character, so that the man is truly the result of his past thinking and doing. (v. *Anatta. Ego.*)

For the sub-divisions of the Skandhas see Rh. D. *Buddhism* (S.P.C.K.), pp. 90-93.

Note that each of the Five Skandhas is an aggregate or complex group: each is a *khandha*; i.e., a collection of parts forming a whole.

SOTAPANNA (P): "He who has entered the stream." The first of the Four Paths (q.v.) to liberation. *Sotâpatti*, the state of a sotâpanna, conversion.

SOUL: A term usually avoided by Buddhists to avoid misconception. Bsm does not admit an immortal unchanging entity created by a deity, the destiny of which may be eternal happiness or eternal misery according to the deeds of the personality it ensouls. The "soul" is the character created by experience in the phenomenal worlds, and ever becoming more and more enlightened by following the Path, or more degraded by departing from it. (v. *Ego. Atman. Anatta.*)

STUPA: See *Chaitya. Dagoba.*

SUCHNESS: (v. *Tathata.*)

SUICIDE: According to Buddhist doctrine a man cannot avoid suffering by taking his life, nor can he escape from the "Wheel of Life" by so doing. The destruction of the physical body merely transfers the entity to other spheres of existence, and rebirth into the physical follows. Physical life is considered of great importance, as it is only in the physical that the Way to Liberation can be followed (that is, until the *anagamin* stage is attained). Taking one's life is, therefore, waste of opportunity. Voluntary sacrifice of one's life for the welfare of others is considered meritorious, the motive being an altruistic one. The admonition against suicide in the *Vinaya* applies equally to bhikkhu and layman. "The bhikkhu who preaches, 'End this wretched life, full of suffering and sin; death is better,' preaches murder, is a murderer, is no longer a bhikkhu."

SUKARAMADDAVA: (v. *Boar's flesh*.)

SUKHAVATI (Sk): The Paradise or Pure Land of the Jodo sects of Japan. The "Western Paradise" of Amida. Its glories are described in Oriental metaphor in the two *Sukhavati Vyuha Sutras*. It is also called Sukhâra. *Sukhavati Vyuha* (smaller and larger) are given in English translations in vol. 49 *S.B.E.*

SUNYA (Sk): Void. The doctrine which asserts the transcendental nature of Ultimate Reality. It declares the phenomenal world to be void of a self-substance (*svabhâva*), and the noumenal to be void of all limitations of particularization.

This doctrine abolishes all concepts of dualism and proclaims the essential oneness of the phenomenal and the noumenal.

This doctrine of the "void" is often assumed to be distinctly Mahayana, but this is incorrect. The principle of *sunyata* (voidness) is clearly laid down in the Pali Canon; e.g., *Maj. N.* i, 296-8, explains the attainment of *samadhi* by meditation on the state which is void of phenomenal relations, that state being boundless (*appamâna*), naught (*âkiñcañña*), void (*suññata*), and non-phenomenal (*animitta*). See *Further Dial.* I, 211-213; also *Maj. N.* ii, 261, *Dig. N.* iii, 219. Also Suzuki, *O.M.B.* 173, and *Studies in Lank. S.* 446.

SUTTA (P), SUTRA (Sk): A thread or string (on which jewels are strung), thus applied to that part of the Pali Canon containing the narratives about dialogues by the Buddha. The *Sutta Pitaka* consists of the five "Nikayas," i.e., Digha, Majjhima, Samyutta, Anguttara, Khuddaka. For further details see *APC.*, pp. 3-8 and 16-18. There are also a number of Mahayana scriptures called *sutras*. Sutra of Forty-two Sections: A collection of scripture extracts compiled by the pioneer missionaries to China, 67 A.D. The first Buddhist literature to be trsl. into Chinese. Eng. trsl. *Sermons of a Buddhist Abbot*, pp. 3-21.

SWASTIKA (Sk): The revolving cross, called the Buddhist Cross or the Jaina Cross. It symbolizes the ceaseless activity of the universal life principle evolving the cosmos. Its correct form is 卐 with the arms revolving from right to left. In Bon Tantricism the arms are reversed: this latter form being more correctly called *sauvastika*, and is the symbol of Black Magic.

The swastika is used in China and Japan as the symbol of prosperity and long life.

TANHA (P), TRISHNA (Sk): Thirst for sentient existence. (v. *Desire*.)

TANTRICISM (or TANTRISM): This word covers a vast number of forms developing the innate psychic powers, and of producing magical effects by spells, mantrams, and ceremonial of a variety of kinds. It may be "white" or "black," according to the motives of the performer, and according to the methods used. The subject is so vast, that any attempt at a definition in the limited space at our disposal would be misleading. Suffice to say that the white aspect deals with pure occultism: self-development by *Raja Yoga;* whilst the black, which is concerned with the worship of the female energy in nature, is a licentious form of black magic of the worst kind. We refer readers to the article on Tantrism in *E.R.E.*, vol. 12, pp. 192-197. To the refs. in *Tibetan Book of the Dead, esp.* 213-222. To Arthur Avalon, *Principles of Tantra,* Part I (London, 1914), and to the numerous volumes of translations of the Tantric Literature of India by Sir John Woodroffe (Arthur Avalon).

TAO (Ch): Originally meant "speech." Thus Lao Tzu says: "The Tao that can be *tao*-ed is not the true Tao." Later used by Taoists and Buddhists in rather the same way as the Logos of Greek philos. May be understood as the Way or Law of life which includes the one who lives, life and the relationship between them. Thus to realize Tao in life is to realize one's true meaning, or, in Bdst terms, to realize one's Buddha-nature. (v. *Taoism.*)

TAOISM: One of the three religions of China, said to have been founded by Lao Tzu *circ.* 600 B.C. Its principles are derived mainly from Lao Tzu's book, the *Tao-Te-Ching* and from the writings of Chuang Tzu who lived some 200 years later. Has had great influence on Chinese Bsm, and especially on Zen, q.v.

TATHAGATA (Sk): A title of the Buddha, used by his followers, and also by himself when speaking of himself. Derivation doubtful, and meaning had been lost by time of Buddhaghosa, who gives eight possible meanings.

It is now usually derived from *tathâ-âgata* (thus come), and *tathâ-gata* (thus gone), and given the meaning: He who has come and gone as former Buddhas; i.e., teaching the same truths, and followed the Path to the same Goal.

The M. school prefer: One who has attained full realization of That-ness (*Tathâ-tâ*); i.e., become one with the Absolute (Dharmakaya), so that he "neither comes from anywhere (*na âgamana*), nor goes to anywhere (*na gamana*)." See *Vajracchedika*: *S.B.E.* 49, p. 142.

TATHATA (Sk.): Lit. "Thusness" or "Suchness." Term used in Mahayana for the ultimate and unconditioned nature of life. In one sense it is Sunya (q.v.) expressed positively. It is that which is expressed in all separate things, which is not different from them and which is not divided by them. It cannot be called the One as distinct from the Many, for it is not distinct from anything. Nothing can be denied or affirmed concerning it, for these are modes of expression which exclude and create opposition. It can only be understood when one realizes absolutely that one can neither find it by searching nor lose it by trying to separate oneself from it. And yet it has to be found. For the understanding of Tathata and union with it is Enlightenment. Biblio: Suzuki's *Bsm in Life and Thought of Japan*, London, 1937.

TENDAI: An important Japanese sect founded on the doctrines of the Chinese *T'ien-t'ai* School. The original school was founded by Chih-i in the latter half of the sixth century, and the Japanese sect by Saichi (Dengyo Daishi), c. 805 A.D. Saichi built a monastery on Mt. Hiei, which was for centuries the greatest centre of Buddhist learning in Japan. The outstanding feature of Tendai is its harmonizing tendencies. Realizing to the full the relativity of existence and the limitations of the lower mind, it recognizes all the doctrines of all sects as aspects of the *dharma*; as efforts to bring it within the comprehension of all types of mind. At the same time it views the doctrine as taught in the *Saddharma Pundarika* and the *Suvarnaprabhasa,* as its highest and purest presentation. Tendai reverences the Dhyani Buddha *Vairochana,* whom it identifies with the Amida of the Pure Land Schools, as the supreme source of Truth, the *Buddha Sakayamuni* having received his illumination from him. He, in turn, passed it on to the Lord Maitreya who revealed it to Asanga (v. *Vasubandhu.*) It teaches the Middle Way between *sunya* and *asunya,* seeing the phenomenal as a limited expression of the Real, and the Real as veiled in the phenomenal. Biblio: v. *Japan.*

TEXT: The word "Text" is used by Buddhist scholars to describe a work in its original language: Pali, Sanskrit, Tibetan, Chinese, Japanese, as the case may be. There is a misuse of the term in volume 49 *S.B.E.*, which is often called "Buddhist Mahayana Texts," because this appears on the title page. There are no "Texts" in the volume, and the correct title, "Buddhist Mahayana Sutras," appears on the cover of the volume. The work should always be referred to, therefore, as *Buddhist Mahayana Sutras.*

THEOSOPHY: Wisdom Religion, or Divine Wisdom. Sometimes incorrectly rendered as the "Wisdom of God." The substratum of Truth on which all religions are based; the source from which they derive whatever Truth they contain. The esoteric interpretation of all religious doctrines and dogmas. The various cults and practices now grafted on to certain Theosophical Societies have little in common with the original teaching, for which see *Key to Theosophy* and other works by H. P. Blavatsky (q.v.).

THERA-GATHA and THERI-GATHA: The names of two works of the Pali Canon (*APC.* 275, 276). An important collection of poems or hymns relating the experiences of arahatship. Eng. trsl. *Psalms of the Brethren,* and *Psalms of the Sisters* (P.T.S. 1913 and 1909).

THERAVADA: The "doctrine of the Elders" (who formed the First Buddhist Council). The name applied to the primitive orthodox sect, from which the eighteen Hinayana sects developed. Now often applied to the Hinayana School as a more courteous title than Hinayana.

TIBET: The religion of Tibet is Lamaism, a form of Bsm incorporating pre-Buddhist mythology and spirit-worship on the one hand, and Tantric mysticism on the other. Although thus degraded, it still preserves, as Waddell (*Lamaism*, p. 17) says: "Much of the loftier philosophy and ethics of the system taught by Buddha himself."

Bsm was introduced into Tibet about 640 A.D (there is no evidence to support the tradition that it was introduced by Kasyapa c. 436 A.D.). It made little progress until Padma Sambhava (q.v.) visited Tibet in 749 and founded the Sangha, and also established the ritualistic mysticism of the Yogacharya School. An era of religious activity followed. The Canon was translated into Tibetan, the work being done with remarkable accuracy. Padma Sambhava left Tibet in 802. The religion he established gradually degenerated during the next 200 years, and in 1038 a much-needed Reformation was undertaken by an Indian monk named Atisa. He purged Lamaism of its grosser elements and founded an Order of the more enlightened monks called Kah-dam. His reforms were continued by two of Tibet's greatest saints, Milarepa and Marpa.

Some 350 years later Tsong-kha-pa (1355-1417) made yet greater reforms, and founded the Ge-lug-pa or "Yellow Hat" Order, which in the year 1640 became the State Church, and which consists of the most enlightened minds in the country.

Lamaism—a Western term—is a comprehensive term covering a vast range of religious expression, from the degraded phallism and necromancy of Bön on the one hand, to the most enlightened Buddhist doctrine and practice on the other. The really Buddhist sect is the Ge-lug-pa or "Yellow Hat" sect, and the basic doctrines of this sect vary little from those of the Mahayana School generally. The Supreme Reality is personified as Adi Buddha and is worshipped under his aspect of Amitabha. Divine revelation and power is believed to be conferred on the Tashi Lama who is infallible in doctrinal matters. Ritual is used to raise the consciousness of the devotee to ecstatic states, but stress is also laid on the necessity for a moral life, the doctrine of *karma* being interpreted in a crudely realistic way. The ritual of Lamaism as performed at Lhasa bears strong outward resemblance to that of Roman Catholicism. Bells, rosaries, holy-water, gorgeous vestments and incense all form part. It has fasts and confessions, the worship of the virgin, saints and angels; huge monasteries and a powerful hierarchy, with even an infallible Pope, the representative of Amitabha on earth. There are, however, enlightened men among the higher Lamas who know that all these are outward forms of appealing to the unenlightened mind; crutches for those who cannot walk without their aid.

There are esoteric schools in Tibet, as there are in China and Japan, but little is known about them. H. P. Blavatsky's *Secret Doctrine* gives a great deal of information on the esoteric teachings, and Sinnett's *Esoteric Buddhism* may also be consulted. See Waddell, *The Buddhism of Tibet, or Lamaism*, also *Lhasa and its Mysteries*. Ekai Kawaguchi, *Three Years in Tibet*, the works of Mme. David Neel. Sir Chas. Bell and W. Y. Evans Wentz.

TRIKAYA (Sk): The M. doctrine of the Three Bodies or Trinity, first systematized by Asvaghosa in *A.F.M.* This originally was the doctrine of the basic unity of the Reality underlying manifestation, the phenomenal or Nirmanakaya, and the noumenal or Sambhogokaya, being aspects of the One Ultimate Reality, the Dharmakaya, one in essence with *Tathata* (q.v.).

From this developed the doctrine of the transcendental Buddha, who, as Dharmakaya, is one in essence with the basic unity of Being, but who manifests as an Avatar for the saving of humanity, his physical body being a purely illusory one. (v. *Saddharma Pundarika.*)

As applied to the development of Buddhahood and Bodhisattva-hood, the doctrine teaches that each aspirant for Buddha-hood may, on attaining the Goal, renounce final Nirvana and keep in touch with humanity by dwelling in the Nirmanakaya, through which he may function at will on any of the phenomenal planes of existence, the Sambhogakaya being the vehicle of the Divine Power of the Dharmakaya. See *Voice of the Silence,* Part III, note 34 (p. 95 Peking ed.).

TSONG-KHA-PA (or JE-RIN-PO-CH'E): A great Tibetan reformer (1355-1417). He built the Gahldan Monastery, near Lhasa, and founded the Ge-lug-pa or "Yellow Hat" sect there. This sect aims at the purification of Lamaism from its Bon and Tantric elements, and to it belong the most enlightened minds of Tibet, including both the Tashi and the Dalai Lamas.

UDANA: A "breathing out," an "exultant cry." The utterance of an inspired thought. The title of one of the oldest works in the Pali Pitakas. See APC. 265. Trsl. into English: *The Udana, or the Solemn Utterances of the Buddha.* D. M. Strong. Luzac (1902).

UNCONSCIOUS: A term used by Dr. D. T. Suzuki to translate the Chinese *wu-hsin,* lit. "no mind" or "no thought." This does not mean mere vacuity, but rather freedom from attachment to thoughts. This should be distinguished from the Unconscious of modern psychology, which is less a state of mind (as *wu-hsin*) than a collection of mental contents unknown to the conscious "ego." (v. *Viññana.*)

UPADANA (P): Clinging to existence: the "will to live." That which supports existence. The ninth link in the Chain of Existence. (v. *Nidamas.*)

UPASAKA (P): A lay disciple who strives to keep the Five Precepts at all times, and the Eight Precepts on Uposatha days, and who tries to follow the Eightfold Path so far as is possible whilst living in the world. The feminine form is *upasika.*

UPOSATHA (P): The 1st, 8th, 15th, and 23rd days of the lunar month; i.e., Full Moon, New Moon and the days equi-distant between them. They were kept as fast days in pre-Buddhist times, and were utilized by the early Buddhists as days for special meetings of the Order, for recitation of Patimokkha, etc. They became recognized as "sabbath" days, or days for expounding or listening to the *dhamma*, for keeping special precepts, etc., and are still recognized for that purpose in most Buddhist lands.

VACCHAGOTTA: A wandering ascetic who questioned the Buddha on certain metaphysical problems (the indeterminates), especially those relating to the ego and the state of the *arahat* after death. Related in the *Aggi-Vacchagotta Sutta* (*APC.* 106), quoted in full in Warren, *Buddhism in Trsl.*, p. 123 sqq.

VEDANA (P): Sense reaction to contact. The seventh link in the Chain of Causation, producing the craving or thirst for existence. The body of feeling or sensation, the second of the Five Skandhas.

VEDANTA: The end or consummation of the doctrine of the Vedas. One of the six orthodox systems of Hindu philosophy. Teaches the panentheistic doctrine of the Brahman as the Reality unifying all phenomena, and the identity of man's real Self with that ultimate Reality. Nothing

Real exists outside Brahman: "There is One only, without a second." This doctrine is set forth in a variety of forms in the scriptures called Upanishads. Its chief exponent was Sankara (charya) c. 800 A.D.

Like Bsm. Vedanta starts from primal ignorance and asserts that Enlightenment comes from the realization of the innate divinity of man. This is gained by experience through numbers of incarnations. The Vedanta is expressed in two forms based on the recognition of absolute truth and relative truth. The former (*parâ vidyâ*) gives the esoteric teaching, the latter (*aparâ vidyâ*) the popular empirical point of view. The former postulates Brahman as void of all attributes (*nirguna*). [cp. Mahayana "sunya" doctrine], the latter endows Brahman with attributes of personality (*saguna*) for the purpose of bringing the finite mind into a receptive attitude for its development towards enlightenment. Mahayana Bsm has been influenced by Vedanta conceptions, and an acquaintance with its ideas is essential for a study of the Mahayana. See Max Müller, *Vedanta Philosophy* (London, 1894). Radhakrishnan, *Indian Philosophy*.

VIHARA: A dwelling-place or abode. Also a state of life or condition (of heart) v. *Brahma viharas*. The houses presented to the Buddha for the use of the Sangha were called *viharas*, and the name is now usually applied to any Buddhist retreat or monastery.

VINAYA: The Vinaya Pitaka is the third main division of the Tipitaka. It is concerned with the Rules of Discipline governing the Sangha. It is divided into (1) *Suttavibhanga* dealing with patimokkha (q.v.), (2) *Khandhakas*, sub-divided into *Mahavagga* and *Cullavagga*, and (3) *Parivara*, summaries and classifications of the Rules, arranged for instruction and examination purposes. See APC., p. 9. Eng. trsl. *S.B.E.*, vols. xiii, xvii, xx. The

Mahavastu (q.v.) also contains a Vinaya section (*Vinayavastu*) which contains the Vinaya Rules of the Mahasanghikas (q.v.).

VINNANA (P), VIJNANA (Sk): As one of the Five Skandhas Viññâna is the normal consciousness, the relation between subject and object. It is the empirical mind, the vehicle (*upadhi*) by which one cognizes the phenomenal worlds and gains the experience of life.

Viññâna is also the consciousness which lies below the threshold of normal experience (the subliminal consciousness), in which the experiences of the past are registered and retained, the results of such experience becoming faculties in the next physical birth. This is Viññâna as a link in the Chain of Causation, where it is described as the creation of the *Sankharas* (these here including sensation (*vedana*) and awareness of sensation (*sañña*), and is in its turn the cause of *Nama-Rupa* (mind and form)). See *Digha II*, 63 (*Dial. II*, 60).

It is thus a "Causality Body," a storehouse of Causes and Effects: a link between personalities.

Here we are encroaching into the region of metaphysics where speculation in the different schools has been rife, each trying to expound some theory of a connection between the various personalities, which at the same time does not conflict with the *anatta* doctrine. The Hinayana Sammitiyas, for example, taught a transmigrating entity (the *Vijñanavadakaya*) which was superior to the *skandhas*, but was not an ego or self. Certain Mahayana schools postulated the *ativahika* or subtle "transporting body" which linked the consciousness at death to the consciousness at rebirth. The Tibetan Yoga schools assert that behind or beyond the 27 elements of the Skandhas stands the sub-consciousness of *viññâna* as "Knower," the innate Reality awakened to self-consciousness by phenomenal experience, the "Self" which attains Nirvana. The esoteric schools teach that Viññâna is dual, the "lower" being the viññâna of the *skandhas*, functioning in the worlds of the senses and disintegrating after the death of the lower vehicles, whilst the "higher" is the intuitional mind, or the mind illuminated by *bodhi* (*buddhi*), the seat of *prajña*, transcendental wisdom. As the Buddha himself expressed it, in the *Lankavatara Sutra*: "This is the Reality that endures, it is the realm beyond the ken of discrimination: it is the mind itself, but freed from the entanglements of speculation and imagination; and it reveals itself through our empirical consciousness when our empirical consciousness goes beyond itself, that is, when it transcends dualism."

This viññâna is no "soul," however, for "that light which shines within thee, differs in no wise from the light which shines in thy brother-men. It is the personality under the illusion of *attavada*, which says, 'my soul and thy soul.'"

v. *Citta. Mano.*

VISUDDHI MAGGA: Title of a famous work on Buddhist doctrine by Buddhaghosa. Trsl. into English by Pe Maung Tin. *The Path of Purity.* Pali Text Society. Part I (1923), Pt. II (1930).

VOICE OF THE SILENCE: A translation by H. P. Blavatsky of portions of a work called the "Book of the Golden Precepts," which is used for the instruction of disciples in the occult Buddhist schools. The first edition, published 1889, is now unobtainable, but various later editions are on sale, notably a reprint published by the Chinese Buddhist Research Society, Peking, in 1927, with a foreword by the Tashi Lama. Another smaller edn. is published by the United Lodge of Theosophists.

WESAK, or VESAK (Sinhalese), VAISAKHA (Sk): The month corresponding to April-May, on the Full-Moon Day of which is celebrated the Birth, Renunciation, Enlightenment and Parinibbana of the Buddha. The festival is called "Wesak" from the name of the month. If there are two Full-Moon days in the month of May, the first is the Wesak Day. The Japanese Mahayana sects celebrate the Birth of the Buddha on April 8th.

WHEEL OF LIFE (*Bhavachakra*): The Wheel has been used by many religions as the symbol of the ever-rolling activity of life. Buddhism adopted the same symbol to typify the ceaseless process of becoming and its limitation (finiteness). It conceives of man as bound to this Wheel so long as he thinks of him(self) as bound, but when he attains a realization that the ".self" he thinks of is an illusory "self," he is freed from the Wheel and attains liberation into that state of infinity called Nirvana.

The Tibetans make great use of pictorial representations of the Wheel to bring before the mind the nature of existence. It is based on the Twelve Nidanas, its six sections portraying the different spheres of existence in which the concatenation of Cause and Effect operates. The six spheres are: the Heaven worlds, the Asura worlds, the Human worlds, the Animal worlds, the Purgatorial worlds, and the Hells. It is noteworthy that in the lowest hell there is an exit, and that a Buddha is depicted in each of the six worlds, thus indicating that he is ever ready to aid in whatsoever state one may be. The Wheel is depicted as being whirled round by a demon, this symbolizing the miseries and limitations of existence, and in the centre of the wheel are shown the three cardinal sins or blemishes of character; lust, malevolence, and stupidity-greed, symbolized by the red cock, the green snake, and the black pig. Outside the wheel the Buddha is depicted, to symbolize release from the Wheel as the *summum bonum*, and his attainment thereof.

Illustrations and descriptions of the "Wheel" appear in volumes five and six of *Buddhism in England*.

Praying wheel: A mechanical device for repeating invocations: used in Tibet. See Simpson, *The Buddhist Praying Wheel* (London, 1896).

Wheel of the Law: The *dhamma* as an ever-rolling chariot wheel: the symbol of conquering efficacy; the Buddha being the *Dhamma-cakkavattin* or Universal Monarch in the domain of Righteousness. The preaching of the First Sermon at Benares is called the *Dhamma-cakkappavatana-sutta*, or the Discourse of setting in motion the Chariot Wheel of the Good Law.

The Wheel of the Law, Alabaster: The standard work on Siamese Buddhism.

"WHEEL, THE." Organ of the British Maha Bodhi Society. A mimeographed, monthly publication, which replaced the *British Buddhist* in Janu-Scripture. Engilsh versions by M. Müller, Wood-ary, 1935. Price 4d.

WILL: the word *cetana* was used to mean mind as inclination in action, implying purpose or intention, and is the nearest equivalent to our word "will." The regulation and cultivation of the will was the all-important aim in Buddhism (see Rh. D. in *Dial.* I, xxvi), its cultivation being entirely a matter of ethics. The more a man identified himself with the whole of life (*anatta* in practice), the freer he became, until with the elimination of the *asavas*, the way to complete removal of every fetter was open, and perfect freedom and enlightenment was attained. (v. *Freewill*). Also see *The Will in Bsm.* J.R.A.S. 1898, p. 47.

WISDOM (Prajña): The supreme virtue in Buddhism, it being synonymous with the attainment of Truth in its fullness. It implies not mere knowledge of phenomenal things, but insight into the real nature of existence. It includes knowledge, intuition, compassion.

WOMEN: Bsm has always aimed at the ideal relationship between men and women. The Sangha was established for women as soon as the time was ripe, and regulations were provided for their protection. In Buddhist lands to-day the woman is treated as the equal of man, so far as social conditions permit. A Roman Catholic writer (W. S. Lilly) has, indeed, said: "Buddhism raised women to an elevation never before attained by her in the Oriental world." See Fielding Hall, *Soul of a People*, also Dudley Wright, *Bsm and Women*. *B.R.* III, 243.

Women played an important part in the spread of early Bsm, both as lay disciples and *bhikkhus*. Famous women in early Bsm were: Bhadda, famous for her discourses, and for her memories of former lives: Visakha, a wealthy patroness of the Order: Ambapali, a courtesan who became a convert and supported the Sangha: Dhammadina, the great preacher: Mahapajati, the Buddha's foster-mother, who founded the Sangha for women: Khema, the consort of King Bimbisara, renowned for her profound insight. Yashodhara, the wife of Gotama, also entered the Sangha. In later times we have Sanghamitta, the daughter of Asoka, founding the Sangha in Ceylon. See Mrs. Rh. D., *Psalms of the Sisters* (P.T.S., 1909), and Horner, *Women under Primitive Bsm* (Routledge, 1930).

YAMAKA: A bhikkhu who had been deluded by the "wicked heresy" that the arahat is annihilated after death. Sariputta convinces him of his error. Related in *Sam. N.* xxii, 85. Quoted in full, and commented on by Holmes in *Creed of Buddha*, 186-195. *Yamaka*: The "Book of Pairs." The sixth of the seven works composing the Abhidhamma Pitaka.

YASHODHARA: The wife of Gautama. Also called Gopa.

YOGA: A word meaning "yoke," in the sense of "that which unites," therefore "union" and the system of discipline which brings a man to union (with Reality). There are two great systems: Hatha Yoga, psycho-physiological training along ascetic lines, and Raja Yoga, the development of inner powers by meditation, etc.

YOGACHARYA: An idealistic school of Mahayana which taught that the phenomenal universe is the expression of the essence of mind in eternal evolution.

YOGAVACHARA'S MANUAL: Title of Pali and Sinahalese work on Yoga practices. Eng. trsl. *The Manual of a Mystic,* F. L. Woodward (Pali Text Society, 1916).

ZA-ZEN (Jap): Sitting meditation as practised in Zen Buddhist monasteries. Posture used is the same as for Yoga, but the method of breathing is different and the mental technique is to concentrate on some Ko-an (q.v.). *Za-zen* is usually practised in the meditation hall (*zendo*), and a full account will be found in Suzuki's *Training of the Zen Buddhist Monk,* Kyoto, 1936.

ZEN (Jap): A Chinese and Japanese school of Buddhism which has been described as "the revolt of the Chinese mind" against the Buddhism of India. It evolved from the teaching of Bodhidharma, said to be the Buddha's 28th successor, who came to China in A.D. 527. The word Zen is the Japanese equivalent of the Chinese *Ch'an* or *Ch'an-na,* a corruption of the Sk. *dhyana,* usually translated as "meditation." This, however, gives an erroneous conception of the meaning of Zen, for Zen cannot be confined to any particular practice. Although meditation (v. *Za-zen*) is a part of Zen training, Zen itself includes every possible form of activity. For the Chinese mind wished above all things to apply Bsm to everyday life, asserting that Enlightenment could be found just as much by working in the world as in withdrawing from it in the Indian manner.

Zen is therefore described as:—

A special transmission of Enlightenment outside the Scriptures;
No dependence on words and letters;
Direct pointing to the soul of man;
Seeing into one's own nature, and the attainment of Buddhahood.

Bodhidharma had taught that as all things are Buddhas from the very beginning, the only reason for our not realizing our "Buddha-nature," our perfect harmony and unity with life, was our own ignorance. As man's original nature is this "Buddha-nature," Zen is therefore the simple act of discovering what oneself is. It places no reliance on doctrines and the written word, because these are only ideas *about* Truth and not Truth itself. This Truth of "Buddha-nature" exists in life; therefore Zen points directly at life, and does not consist in ideas *about* life. All the time we are living this Truth; we cannot avoid it, because it *is* ourselves, and if we search for it we cannot find it because the very act of searching obscures the fact that we already have it. It is like trying to see one's own eyes. Zen therefore asks us to give up avoiding and searching alike, and just to "go straight ahead" in the knowledge that there is nothing to strive for and that, in the words of Hui-neng, "the only difference between a Buddha and an ordinary man is that the one realizes he is a Buddha and the other does not." This can only be done when the futility of searching and avoiding has been fully realized, and this Zen effects by means of the Ko-an (q.v.), a form of problem which so intensifies our searching that in the end we see that we are only chasing ourselves.

This teaching cannot be grasped by the ordinary intellectual mind, and therefore Zen literature seems nonsense to merely rational understanding. But its illogical technique is simply a means of jolting the mind out of its ordinary ruts, for purely logical thought leads us in circles.

Zen has had profound influence on Far-Eastern culture. In one sense it is a synthesis of Bsm, Taoism and Confucianism, and as such has penetrated into every department of life, especially into art. In Japan it has strongly influenced the military arts, as *Ju-jutsu* and *Ken-jutsu* (fencing), for the "dynamic immediacy" of its contact with life appealed especially to the warriors (*samurai*). Bibliography: *Intro. to Zen Buddhism*, D. T. Suzuki, Kyoto, 1934. *The Spirit of Zen*, Alan Watts, London, 1936. *Essays in Zen Buddhism*, 3 vols., Suzuki, London, 1927, 1933 and 1934. *The Spirit of Zen* contains a list of all works on the subject in European languages.

Zen has had profound influence on Far Eastern culture. In one sense it is a synthesis of [illegible] Taoism and Confucianism, and as such has penetrated into every department of life, especially into art. In Japan it has strongly influenced the military arts, as *Jiu-jitsu* and *Ken-jutsu* (fencing), for the "dynamic immediacy" of its contact with life appealed especially to the warriors (*Samurai*). Bibliography: *Intro. to Zen Buddhism*, D. T. Suzuki, Kyoto, 1934. *The Spirit of Zen*, Alan Watts, London, 1936. *Essays in Zen Buddhism*, 3 vols., Suzuki, London, 1927, 1933 and 1934. *The Spirit of Zen* contains a list of all works on the subject in European languages.